The Bat Mitzvah Treasury

A collection of illumination, calligraphy,
inspiring messages, essays and laws
for the young woman
as she becomes Bat Mitzvah

By
Rabbi Yonah Weinrib

The Bat Mitzvah Treasury

Published by

Judaica Illuminations, Ltd.

Distributed by

Mesorah Publications, ltd

איכה
בקרת מעוד

Illumination, calligraphy, commentary
and insights by
Rabbi Yonah Weinrib

First Edition, First Impression ... October 2004

Published by Judaica Illuminations Ltd.

1664 Coney Island Ave. • Brooklyn, NY 11230 • 718-375-4600
www.judaicailluminations.com

Distributed by Mesorah Publications, Ltd.

4401 Second Avenue • Brooklyn, NY 11232 • 718-921-9000 • www.artscroll.com

Distributed in Israel by
SIFRIATI / A. GITLER
6 Hayarkon Street
Bnei Brak 51127, Israel

Distributed in Europe by
LEHMANNS
Unit E, Viking Industrial Park, Rolling Mill Rd.
Jarrow, Tyne and Wear, NE32 3DP, England

Distributed in Australia and New Zealand by
GOLDS WORLD OF JUDAICA
3-13 William Street
Balaclava, Melbourne 3183, Victoria, Australia

Distributed in South Africa by
KOLLEL BOOKSHOP
Shop 8A Norwood Hypermarket
Norwood 2196, Johannesburg, South Africa

ISBN: 1-57819-311-7
Printed in Canada

ARTIST, WE'RE JUST BRUSHES IN HIS HAND, IF ALL THE SKIES WERE PARCHMENT AND THE HILLS WERE MADE OF TREES, AND THE אומן TO WRITE THE LETTERS WAS THE WATER OF THE SEAS, AND THE PEOPLE OF CREATION WERE THE SCRIBES TO WRITE THE TALE, THEY COULD NEVER, EVER, tell THE GLORY OF THE GOD OF YISRAEL, FOR IT'S HE WHO PAINTS THE PICTURE, WE JUST FOLLOW HIS COMMAND, FOR HASHEM'S THE ARTIST

Table of Contents

Acknowledgments

With the completion of the Bat Mitzvah Treasury, a work in progress has been completed. Transitions was the name of a previous title on Bat Mitzvah, a project I worked on in the collection with dear friend and colleague, Rabbi Yaakov Salamon. The first offering on the subject shared messages and artwork that laid the foundation for this endeavor. In Judaism, we know there is no such thing as coincidence. The conception of that volume took place in 1992, and now — almost exactly twelve years later — we celebrate the book's Bat Mitzvah.

The point in common between the two works focuses as well on the celebrants themselves. Morad and Diana Roshanzamir, a prominent family in the Persian community, initiated the project on Bat Mitzvah for their daughter, Jessica. Joseph and Judy Weil extended the scope of Transitions to include the many items included in the Bat Mitzvah Treasury. This beautiful and meaningful keepsake was created for their daughter, and can now be shared with thousands of young ladies celebrating their special day. A special mazel tov to Joseph and Judy on the Bat Mitzvah of their daughter — Jessica.

Bat Mitzvah is a particularly challenging subject to explore. A young woman's obligation to perform mitzvot at twelve parallels the young man's requirement to uphold commandments at thirteen, both of which were given to Moses at Mount Sinai. There is little said about Bar Mitzvah and even less on Bat Mitzvah, though in truth they are watershed events in the lives of young men and women, respectively. What is significant for today's young woman, to help imbue her with a sense of purpose and inspiration now that she has come of age?

As there are few specific *halachot* that pertain to the twelve-year-old celebrant, it was deemed appropriate to address the areas that pertain particularly to Jewish women. Areas of Jewish thought, Jewish law specific to the Jewish woman, prayer, *Rosh Chodesh* and various aspects of *chesed*, lovingkindness, would address personal observance and communal responsibility. Before she becomes Bat Mitzvah, her actions may be confined to a limited sphere of influence; now that she has attained majority status, her impact is far greater. Hopefully, the inspiration gained will enable her to make herself a better person, and the world a better world.

The foundations that were laid twelve years ago with Rabbi Yaakov Salamon as we worked on Transitions have given the Bat Mitzvah Treasury its basic structure. Having been privileged to work with him on other projects has greatly enabled me to benefit from his creativity, learning and profound sensitivity. His imprint is found throughout this volume. Bat Mitzvah, particularly because it deals with a young girl becoming a young lady, requires warmth, understanding and a vision into the soul of those young women. Mrs. Baila Sheva Brenner's

What is significant for today's young woman, to help imbue her with a sense of purpose and inspiration now that she has come of age?

literary expertise has beautifully captured the tone in the sections on Role Models and *Chesed*. Her writing and editing on other sections of the volume enhanced it tremendously. In Judaism, having an understanding of the theoretical relevance of a subject without being familiar with its practical application leaves one ungrounded. I am particularly grateful to my dear son, Rabbi Avi Weinrib, who has clearly and succinctly dealt with the laws of candle-lighting, challah, prayer and time-bound *mitzvot*. As with our earlier collaboration in the Shabbos Shiron, it was a nachas-filled endeavor. May he continue to learn and grow, and share his talents for Torah dissemination.

The information on *tzniut* was adapted from works by Gila Manelson and Rebbetzin Tzipporah Heller on the subject. While it is only possible to touch upon some important aspects of the subject in a work like this, it bears further study by the reader. The specific *halachic* parameters should be dealt with together with one's rabbi. It would be remiss of me not to include a brief section on a subject which is such a fundamental concept in Judaism in a work on Bat Mitzvah.

The typesetting of Shloimie Nussbaum has helped take my (often inscrutable) longhand into its preliminary typeset form, accurately and patiently. Yaakov Gerber and Yitzchok Saftlas of Bottom Line Design have once again shared their creative computer graphics and professional expertise to enhance my artistic images. Mrs. Tova Finkelman assisted in editing the manuscript, and offered many constructive suggestions to allow for greater facility in reading.

I have been particularly fortunate to have been associated with the ArtScroll family for many years. From David and Elliot Schwartz of ArtScroll Printing, I have learned about many aspects of technical production and the printing industry. From Rabbi Meir Zlotowitz and Rabbi Nosson Scherman, two of the most prolific disseminators of Torah today, I have learned so much about the meaningful interplay of literary artistry and visual aesthetics. ArtScroll has set the standard in Jewish publishing, and each of their works is another gem in the crown of Torah. I echo the sentiments of thousands worldwide in offering my blessings that they continue their magnificent contributions to add treasures of Jewish learning.

I am fortunate to be able to learn from some masters of inspiration and learning. My esteemed Rav, HoRav Eliezer Ginsburg, שליט״א, and the encyclopedic knowledge of my Rebbe, HoRav Shmuel Yosef Lercher, שליט״א, have taught volumes, in text and in character, at our *Bais Hamedrash,* Agudath Israel Snif Zichron Shmuel. I am privileged to learn lessons of Torah and lessons for living from two Torah luminaries, HoRav Avrohom Schorr, שליט״א, and HoRav Elya Brudny, שליט״א. My foundations in learning and love for Torah are a credit to the Yeshiva of Hartford, Talmudical Yeshiva of Philadelphia, Mirrer Yeshiva of Brooklyn and Jerusalem. May I be a worthy disciple to share the lessons of Torah that their selfless Rebbeim have taught.

I thank You for the hand to faithfully transcribe that which You have shown me. May I be worthy of being a brush in the Hand of God.

Though talent is a God-given gift, it has to be nurtured and developed. I owe a tremendous debt of gratitude to the heavenly emissaries who help me share my vision of beautiful and meaningful Judaica. I am grateful for the confidence they have in me to faithfully translate subtle messages into visual images on profound Torah texts.

Helene שתחי' and Zyg ע"ה Wolloch commissioned the calligraphy and commentary of the Haggadah in memory of the Holocaust.

I owe a debt of gratitude to Ira and Ingeborg Rennert and Diana and Morad Roshanzamir. They commissioned the books *Bar Mitzvah: Its Observance and Significance,* and *Transitions,* our earlier volume on Bat Mitzvah, respectively. These have enhanced the understanding of these celebrations, giving them additional meaning.

Rachel and Jack Gindi are patrons of the original scrolls of the *Megillot of Redemption* series on the Five Megillot. Lenore and Stanley Weinstein have helped share the beauty of King David's *tefillot* with the commissioning and publication of *Hallel.* Mr. and Mrs. Rudolph Tessler have embarked with me on a work-in-progress. *Letters of Eternity: The Aleph-Bais Treasury,* has evolved into a comprehensive *magnum opus, The Illuminated Torah* on the Five Books of Moses. Hopefully, it will share the teachings of our Sages in a majestic setting of illumination, calligraphy and commentary. Fred and Cheryl Halpern join me in illuminating the *berachot* in their family heirloom edition, *Shaarei Berachah.*

A special note of appreciation to dear friends Harvey שיחי', and Naomi Wolinetz ע"ה, who commissioned my largest work to date, Pirkei Avot/Ethics of the Fathers. In the three and one-half years it took to complete the original manuscript, and with the publication of the Collector's Edition and popular editions, we have been humbled by the response. May it continue to enlighten and inspire.

My beloved parents, Mr. and Mrs. Chaim Weinrib שיחיו, my dear father-in-law, Rav Leib Isbee, זצ"ל, and יבל"ח, my mother-in-law, Mrs. Rose Isbee, תחי', deserve my eternal gratitude. They have been inspirational role models and teachers to our family, transmitting the beauty of our heritage to their children.

My wife, Miriam, partner in my every endeavor, role model and inspiration for our family, continues to teach lessons for life to our family and her many dear friends. May we continue to enjoy *nachat* from our wonderful children and grandchildren, and may our *tefillot* be answered.

And to the Master Artist who has given me a gift. I thank You for the heart to be sensitive to the beauty of Your creations; I thank You for the eyes that at times see that which may be hidden from others; I thank You for the mind to comprehend in some measure the depth of Your Torah; and I thank You for the hand to faithfully transcribe that which You have shown me. May I be worthy of being a brush in the Hand of God.

Yonah Weinrib

Cheshvan 5765

Transmission:

From Parents to Children

Parents' Message

אוֹדֶה ה' בְּכָל-לִבִּי (תהלים ט:ב)
"I will thank G-d with all my heart." (Psalms 9:2)

Becoming Bat Mitzvah is a very special time in the life of a young woman. It's a time for reflection and contemplation, looking back at past accomplishments and forward to the challenges and successes that life will hopefully bring. But most of all, it's a time to express profound gratitude to the Almighty for bringing us to this wonderful milestone in our lives.

The Bat Mitzvah is not merely an obligation to be mindful of one's lineage. It is much more. It is an opportunity to demonstrate the paramount importance of continuing a legacy that has kept the Jewish people alive through the millennia. Despite extreme hardship, overwhelming duress and even persecution and discrimination, the eternal flame of faith has never been extinguished. Your ancestors did not lose sight of the standards and virtues that have maintained us as a strong and vibrant people.

There are many lessons that you are taught in school, but the teachings of your parents, your family, your rabbis and your peers may last long after the memory of your math and history exams have faded. The lessons are subtle but powerful. These are the values, ethics and moral conduct that perhaps can only be taught by example. Honesty, integrity, humility, patience and diligence are character traits that will be important to you in life, and these can be best acquired by being an astute observer. Watch your teachers, carefully seek out positive role models, and learn from the timeless lessons of Judaism's sages. The wellsprings of knowledge are open for you to draw

The Bat Mitzvah is an opportunity to demonstrate the paramount importance of continuing a legacy that has kept the Jewish people alive through the millennia.

from; the resources can be made available, but it is up to you to use them.

We live in an age of technological sophistication. At the touch of a dial or the flick of a switch, we can be exposed to the best — and the worst — that life has to offer, It's all there for you to see, but you must take care to be discerning. You can learn the beautiful messages of life if you filter out the negative influences that are so pervasive, and treasure the teachings of those who can guide you through life.

For the Sake of the Children

It is told that when G-d was about to bestow the Torah upon the Jewish people, there was much consternation in the heavens above. "Al-mighty G-d," the angels pleaded, "You are about to give away Your most sacred treasure, the Torah, and yet what guarantors do You have for its safekeeping?" G-d considered the words of the angels and found them to be just. But what could mere mortals offer the Creator of the Universe? What guarantees could they possibly give?

There were those who counseled that the prophets, the sages and the rabbis be held as surety. But G-d did not accept them.

There were those who advised that the Patriarchs and the Matriarchs, the ancestors of our nation, act as guarantors, but still G-d did not accept them.

Finally it was suggested that the children offer to act as guarantors for the nation. Immediately, G-d assented and gave the Torah to the Jewish people as an eternal inheritance.

Our children, then, are not simply our offspring: they are the guarantors of our survival, the links to our future, and, as our Sages taught, the builders of our world *(Midrash)*.

As a Bat Mitzvah, you are the next link in the glorious chain of our heritage. We feel confident that you will be faithful to the obligations and responsibilities worn proudly by every *bat Yisrael,* daughter of Israel, as she embarks on the road to adulthood. Use each of your G-d-given gifts to the fullest, becoming the person that only you can be.

May G-d grant you a long, happy and healthy life, and your family many years and opportunities to see the beauty of your development. May you grow in body, mind, spirit, and

Life is a series of transitions. Each stage flows into the next, as your childhood passes and another chapter of our life is about to be written.

character and always be able and eager to help those around you. Continue on the path of righteousness and remain cognizant of your responsibilities to G-d, your people, your family and yourself. This will assure you of happiness and deep satisfaction, for many years to come.

Life is a series of transitions. Each stage flows into the next, as your childhood passes and another chapter of our life is about to be written. You move on, imbued with a sense of purpose and commitment, dedicated to the beautiful Torah ideals you've learned over the years.

Go confidently — because our love and support will always be with you.

Be steadfast — for your determination to succeed will hold you in good stead.

Look back—and cherish your past years, and the generations who have given you so much to help make you who you are today,

Look forward — for the goals and aspirations you seek will help you reach every tomorrow.

With all our love,
Your mother, father and family

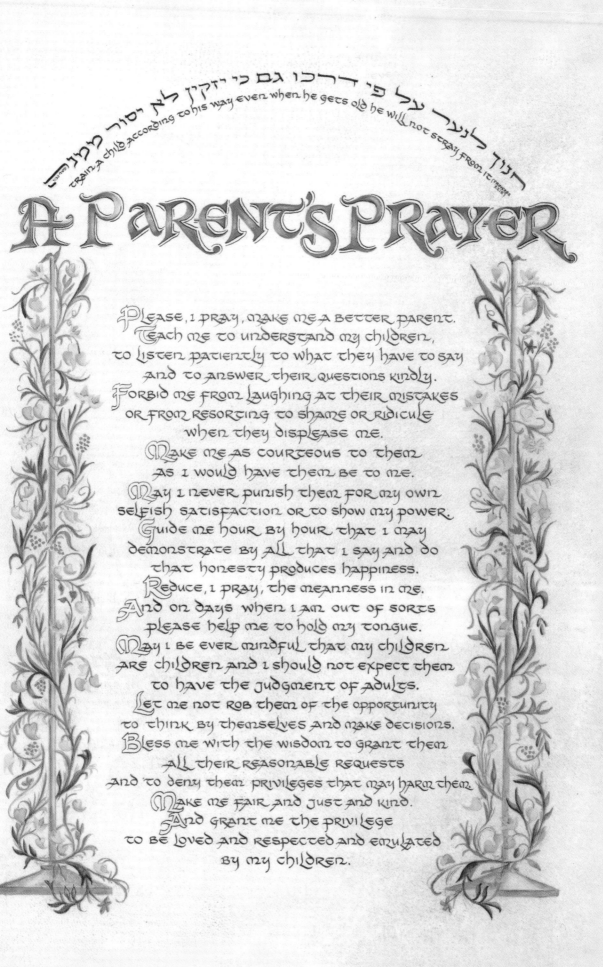

על פי דרכו גם כי יזקין לא יסור ממנה חנך לנער

TRAIN A CHILD ACCORDING TO HIS WAY EVEN WHEN HE GETS OLD HE WILL NOT STRAY FROM IT

A PARENT'S PRAYER

Please, I pray, make me a better parent.
Teach me to understand my children,
to listen patiently to what they have to say
and to answer their questions kindly.
Forbid me from laughing at their mistakes
or from resorting to shame or ridicule
when they displease me.
Make me as courteous to them
as I would have them be to me.
May I never punish them for my own
selfish satisfaction or to show my power.
Guide me hour by hour that I may
demonstrate by all that I say and do
that honesty produces happiness.
Reduce, I pray, the meanness in me.
And on days when I am out of sorts
please help me to hold my tongue.
May I be ever mindful that my children
are children and I should not expect them
to have the judgment of adults.
Let me not rob them of the opportunity
to think by themselves and make decisions.
Bless me with the wisdom to grant them
all their reasonable requests
and to deny them privileges that may harm them.
Make me fair and just and kind.
And grant me the privilege
to be loved and respected and emulated
by my children.

Blessing for the Daughters

A story is told of the *chassid* who came to beseech his Rebbe for a blessing that his son grow to be a Torah scholar. "A blessing? You are asking for a blessing from *me*? Hashem is the source of all blessings, and I am not empowered to bestow blessings upon individuals. But you! You can pray, and *no one* can pray better than you!"

On Friday night as they light the Shabbat candles, Jewish mothers are given the keys to unlock storehouses of goodness for their children. Upon their return from synagogue, Jewish parents bless their children, beseeching God to make them God-fearing and righteous. We pray to God that our daughters emulate the character traits of the Matriarchs, Sarah, Rebecca, Rachel and Leah. Their kindness, their modesty, their compassion and their selflessness made them the role models for future generations of young women.

We bless our daughters that they follow the example of the Matriarchs. As the foundational pillars of our nation, they create the spiritual base for all future generations.

To successfully create the spiritual and emotional environment necessary to sustain a Jewish home, a woman requires more than her merit alone. She brings with her the character traits, the wisdom and the faith that are the legacy of her mother, grandmother and all the generations since the Matriarchs. It is these women who help build her home and provide her with the necessary tools to pass on these characteristics to her descendants.

Any time is appropriate for a parent to bless a child, but our Sages designated Friday night as a particularly auspicious one. It is a time of peace and tranquility. It is a time when the hectic pace of the week is put on hold and the serenity of Shabbat enables us to focus on the blessings of life. Our heritage. Our family. Our community. Our Torah and *mitzvot* ... and especially our children.

As the parent gently places his hand upon the young girl's head, he intones the priestly blessing. We bless our daughter that she be guarded from harm, in a world that has seen so much cruelty and evil. We ask G-d to bestow upon her the blessing of peace, because we know all too well the horrors of war. May G-d's favor be bestowed upon her, for a life of happiness and all good things. We pray that she should grow and develop as a happy and healthy young woman, until she can share her blessings with the next generation.

To successfully create the spiritual and emotional environment necessary to sustain a Jewish home, a woman requires more than her merit alone. She brings with her the character traits, the wisdom and the faith that are the legacy of her mother, grandmother and all the generations since the Matriarchs.

בִּרְכַּת לַבָּנוֹת

יְשִׂימֵךְ אֱלֹהִים
כְּשָׂרָה רִבְקָה רָחֵל וְלֵאָה

יְבָרֶכְךָ יְיָ וְיִשְׁמְרֶךָ
יָאֵר יְיָ פָּנָיו אֵלֶיךָ וִיחֻנֶּךָּ
יִשָּׂא יְיָ פָּנָיו אֵלֶיךָ וְיָשֵׂם לְךָ שָׁלוֹם

Y'SIMAYCH
*Elōhim
k'Soro Rivko
Rochayl v'Layo.*

Y'VORECH'CHO
*Adōnoy v'yishm'recho.
Yo-ayr Adōnoy panov
aylecho vichuneko.
Yiso Adōnoy
panov aylecho
v'yosaym l'cho
sholōm.*

May Hashem
make you like Sarah,
Rebecca, Rachel and Leah.

May Hashem bless you
and safeguard you.

May Hashem illuminate
His countenance to you,
and be gracious to you.

May Hashem lift His
countenance to you and
grant you peace

Blessing for the Daughters

The following prayer captures the sentiments and prayers that parents pray for their daughters. It is customarily said on the eve of Yom Kippur. It was authored by Chaye Adam.

May Hashem make you like Sarah, Rebecca, Rachel and Leah.

May Hashem bless you and safeguard you.

May Hashem illuminate His countenance to you, and be gracious to you.

May Hashem lift His countenance to you and grant you peace.

May it be the will of our Father in Heaven, that He instills in your heart, His love and fear. May the fear of G-d be upon your face all the days of your life, so that you will not sin. May your desire be for Torah and commandments. May your eyes look straightforward, may your mouth speak wisdom, may your heart meditate (with) awe, may your hands be engaged in commandments and may your feet run to do the will of your Father in Heaven.

May He grant you righteous sons and daughters who occupy themselves with Torah and commandments all their days. May your source be blessed, and may He provide for your livelihood in a permissible way with ease and abundance, from His generous hand – and not from the gifts of men; a livelihood that will free you to serve G-d. May you be inscribed and sealed for a long life among the righteous of Israel, Amen.

מִנְהָג לְבָרֵךְ אֶת הַבָּנִים וּבָנוֹת בְּעֶרֶב יוֹם הַכִּיפּוּרִים שֶׁהוּא עֵת רָצוֹן לִפְנֵי הַקָדוֹשׁ בָּרוּךְ הוּא.

תְּפִלָה זֹאת מִסְפֵּר חַיֵי אָדָם מַבִּיעָה אֶת רְצוֹנֵנוּ שֶׁיִהְיוּ בָּנֵינוּ עוֹבְדִים אֶת ה', לוֹמְדֵי תּוֹרָה וּבַעֲלֵי מִידוֹת טוֹבוֹת

יְשִׂמֵךְ אֱלֹקִים כְּשָׂרָה רִבְקָה רָחֵל וְלֵאָה
יְבָרֶכְךָ ה' וְיִשְׁמְרֶךָ:
יָאֵר ה' פָּנָיו אֵלֶיךָ וִיחֻנֶּךָּ:
יִשָּׂא ה' פָּנָיו אֵלֶיךָ וְיָשֵׂם לְךָ שָׁלוֹם:

יְהִי רָצוֹן מִלְפְנֵי אָבִינוּ שֶׁבַּשָּׁמַיִם שֶׁיִתֵּן בְּלִבֵּךְ אַהֲבָתוֹ וְיִרְאָתוֹ. וְתִהְיֶה עַל פָּנַיִךְ כָּל יָמַיִךְ שֶׁלֹא תֶחֶטָאִי. וִיהִי חֶשְׁקֵךְ בַּתּוֹרָה וּבַמִצְוֹת. עֵינַיִךְ לְנֹכַח יַבִּיטוּ, פִּיךְ יְדַבֵּר חָכְמוֹת, וְלִבֵּךְ יֶהְגֶּה אֵמוֹת. יָדַיִךְ יַעַסְקוּ בְמִצְוֹת, רַגְלַיִךְ יָרוּצוּ לַעֲשׂוֹת רְצוֹן אָבִיךְ שֶׁבַּשָּׁמַיִם. יִתֵּן לָךְ בָּנִים וּבָנוֹת צַדִיקִים וְצִדְקָנִיוֹת עוֹסְקִים בַּתּוֹרָה וּבְמִצְוֹת כָּל יְמֵיהֶם. וִיהִי מְקוֹרֵךְ בָּרוּךְ. וְיַזְמִין לָךְ פַּרְנָסָתֵךְ בְּהֶתֵר וּבְרֶוַח, מִתַּחַת יָדוֹ הָרְחָבָה, וְלֹא עַל יְדֵי מַתְּנַת בָּשָׂר וָדָם. פַּרְנָסָה שֶׁתִּהְיִי פְּנוּיָה לַעֲבוֹדַת ה'. וְתִכָּתְבִי וְתֵחָתְמִי לְחַיִים טוֹבִים וַאֲרוּכִים בְּתוֹךְ כָּל צַדִיקֵי יִשְׂרָאֵל. אָמֵן.

Chinuch— Sharing and Caring for Children

חֲנֹךְ לַנַּעַר עַל־פִּי דַרְכּוֹ גַּם כִּי־יַזְקִין לֹא־יָסוּר מִמֶּנָּה (משלי כב:ו).

each a child according to his ways, even when he gets old he will not stray from it (Proverbs, 22:6). Any good educator or parent realizes that it is important to work with a child based on the natural inclination, abilities and interests of the child. His temperament and inherent knowledge will determine the future course of his success.

Chinuch, however, has a greater meaning than training, or teaching. When Jews the world over celebrate the Festival of Lights, Chanukah, חֲנֻכָּה, they rejoice in the rededication of the Holy Temple. The home of G-dliness on this world was defiled by the Syrian-Greeks, and as such was unfit for the Divine Presence to reside there. The abominations and idols were removed, the sanctuary was cleansed and the glorious edifice that adorned Jerusalem was fit for service once again. The *chinuch* that took place in the Chanukah story was consecrating the Holy Temple, making it a fitting receptacle for holiness.

When a *kohen* began his priestly service, he had to start with an inaugural sacrifice. The *minchas chinuch*, the flour offering that initiated his work in the Holy Temple, was the offering brought to start the process of sanctified service for G-d. The Torah understands that it's difficult to maintain the enthusiasm of one's beginnings. Imagine the first day of school, the first time a Bar Mitzvah boy puts on *tefillin*, the first week of marriage. The heightened level of excitement is hard to maintain, but if the beginning is marked in a special way, hopefully the aura of that start will remain.

The Torah (*Devarim* 20:5) discusses those individuals who return from the battlefield. "Any man that built a house but has not begun to live in it, shall return from war."

מִי־הָאִישׁ אֲשֶׁר בָּנָה בַיִת־חָדָשׁ וְלֹא חֲנָכוֹ יֵלֵךְ וְיָשֹׁב לְבֵיתוֹ (דברים כ:ה)

The word חֲנָכוֹ has as its root חנוך, to begin. Rashi interprets the first use of the house as its beginning. If one built the house, but did not yet live in it, he would be distraught lest the opportunity never present itself. *Targum Yonatan ben Uziel* looks at a different aspect of the inauguration of the home, saying that

It's hard to enumerate all the gifts that one receives from parents. It is an outlook on life and perspectives for living. It is the richness of our heritage as Jews, and the ability to grow and develop as people.

it means anyone who built a house but did not put up a *mezuzah* should return home. The beginning of a home, the חנוך that establishes it as a permanent edifice, is the consecration of the building with a *mezuzah*. If the foundation of holiness has not been planted in the home, it is considered incomplete.

So it is with the *chinuch*, the training, of a child. A baby's early years are infused with love so that when he or she gets older, they grow on the strong emotional foundation provided by their parents. As with the *kohen*, or with Chanukah, the consecration of the Holy Temple, the beginnings must be invested with holiness. Even when he is older, this young child, nurtured on such fundamental principles, will not stray from them.

As a Bat Mitzvah, the young lady will receive many gifts. Some will be pretty, some whimsical, some practical (another set of books!), some particularly meaningful. It's hard to enumerate all the gifts that one receives from parents. It is an outlook on life and perspectives for living. It is all the amenities of each day, and the extras that parents shower upon their children. It is the richness of our heritage as Jews, and the ability to grow and develop as people. It's the self-confidence to take steps on our own, and the shoulders to help bear the pains of growing up.

"How does it happen, and *when* did this all take place?" you'll ask. It's true. Rarely does a parent sit their child down and dictate what they should and how to live their lives productively. Lessons are taught more by example than by formal directives. What are the keys to *chinuch*, to training and imparting the most important meanings about life to children?

The word for influence in Hebrew is generally called הַשְׁפָּעָה, *hashpa'ah*. If one has a positive influence on an individual, it is said that he is a good הַשְׁפָּעָה; if one teaches negative behavior, he is called a bad הַשְׁפָּעָה. In *lashon hakodesh*, the Holy Language of Hebrew, the root of each word sheds light on its true meaning. While one might imagine that the root is שֶׁפַע, referring to an abundance of substance being given to the recipient, another interpretation is quite revealing. The root letters שֶׁפַע, or slant, are also at the core of the word (Rav Yaakov Kamenetsky ז״ל).

The process of influence, particularly from parents to children, works from a higher source coming down to a lower one. Whatever the parent does perforce will filter down to the child, for better or for worse. The parent-child/giver-taker relationship shares as axiomatic the fact that what the parents do greatly affects their children. Subtle lessons about priorities in life, value of time, Torah learning and *mitzvah* observance, and interpersonal relationships are all performed by the parent and trickle down to an impressionable child. The love and respect a child has for a father and mother will be a direct result of how they interchange with each other. A young child is extremely perceptive. What a parent does makes an impression, often long-lasting, on one's children. Honesty, integrity, compassion, diligence and all the virtues of living are taught in the arena we call life.

When the wife of Manoach was expecting a child who would be the leader of the Jewish people, Samson, an angel appeared to her with instructions on how to raise the child. She was told to refrain from drinking wine or eating any foods forbidden to a *nazir*. Samson himself would become a *nazir*, one who does not cut his hair, come in contact with a dead body, or drink wine. When Manoach, who was not present when the angel instructed his wife, pleaded with G-d to let the angel appear once again "to teach us what is to be done with the child to be born." The angel does return, and his prophetic statement is telling.

"Of everything that I spoke to the woman (Manoach's wife) תִּשָּׁמֵר, she should beware" (*Judges* 13:13). He again reiterated the forbidden foods, and ended with a repetitive admonition addressed to his wife, "everything I commanded her תִּשְׁמֹר, she shall observe."

Rav Shimon Schwab ז"ל (*Ma'ayan Beis Hasho'eiva, Parshat Naso*) shares a fascinating insight about parenting. The words תִּשָּׁמֵר and תִּשְׁמֹר mean, *she* should beware and *she* should observe, respectively. In Hebrew grammar, these *same* words, used here in the third-person feminine, are also used in the second-person masculine. "Everything that I commanded her, *you* should beware," תִּשָּׁמֵר. His second admonition, "everything that I commanded her תִּשְׁמֹר," also means "*you* should observe."

Hashem shared, through the angel, the message for parents in every generation, says Rav Schwab. Manoach was told that his child would be a *nazir*, an individual with an elevated level of spirituality. Practices that were common for regular children would be forbidden to him. The child, Samson, had to be different, separate, spiritually superior.

How does one raise a child with such lofty aspirations? The angel answered this unasked question. "Of all these forbidden foods and practices *you* should beware and *you* should observe!" One cannot expect to nurture a holy child in an environment that doesn't foster such exalted behavior. If Manoach would live life on a higher plane, then he could expect great things from his child.

As a Bat Mitzvah, the young girl grows in a home where all the necessities of life, both physical and spiritual, are hopefully provided. She'll learn and she'll grow, incorporating what she's been taught, and flourishing by using her own unique abilities. "One is envious of everything except of one's child and one's student (Talmud, *Sanhedrin* 95b). We pray that our children are better, greater, wiser, more successful than we were. We are confident that all which they achieve in life is built upon the foundations that we've laid for them. On some level, we see ourselves in our children, and hopefully, we'll be proud of them and content with our work. May we, as parents, carry on our exalted mission. May the environment we provide for a budding Bat Mitzvah be steeped in tradition and enhanced by Torah-true values, and enriched with love and warmth.

May our young daughter and all our children bring *nachat* to our family, *nachat* to the Jewish people and *nachat* to her Creator.

Our Rich Jewish Heritage

hat is it that has kept our People alive long after the great empires of the world have vanished from the face of the earth? The Torah tells us that it is not our numbers that make us significant, *"for you are the smallest of all the nations"* (*Deuteronomy 7:7*). Is it not strange that the contributions Jews have made to society in education, the humanities, the arts and sciences are largely disproportionate to our numbers as a people?

For thousands of years we have lived in exile, existing through the benevolence of host countries around the world. We have benefitted from their kindness and contributed to their cultures. But along with our enrichment of their lives, the practices and mores of the secular world have affected our Jewish identity as well. We had to learn to integrate, yet not assimilate; maintaining a delicate balance of two often contrary lifestyles.

This is the backdrop against which one's formative years begin. The challenges, however, become less formidable If one receives direction from parents, support from peers, guidance from teachers, and builds a life predicated on a Torah-true foundation.

Today's young men and women are constantly faced by choices. From the small daily decisions to the major question of values and plans for one's future, they are subjected to crucial, sometimes painful choices.

One might question the need for a set of guidelines for life dictated specifically by the Torah, since we find that there are

We pray that our children are better, greater, wiser, more successful than we were. We are confident that all which they achieve in life is built upon the foundations that we've laid for them.

individuals of moral persuasion in the society at large. Are we then to assume that ethical and moral behavior in Jewish and secular society are one and the same?

In truth, however, the ethical teachings of the Torah and its inherent value system differ greatly from that of the non-Torah culture. Torah values are eternal and immutable, never changing with the fads and styles of the times. *Pirkei Avot*, Ethics of the Fathers, Judaism's most extensive collection of ethical teachings, begins with the saying, "Moses received the Torah at Mount Sinai." The foundation of our ethical beliefs is a timeless set of principles, Divinely handed down to Moses at Mount Sinai. Laws of modesty in dress are determined by *halachic* parameters rather than a Paris designer's fancy; decency, as well as ethical and moral behavior are reflections of Divine decree, not social concurrence. What was seen as permissive in generations past is often seen as puritan today, and the fabric, of contemporary society is comprised of a patchwork of varied values and liberated lifestyles.

Throughout, the Torah and its principles remain eternal. Our leaders, guided by these standards, combine outstanding personal conduct with a high level of scholarship. Adherents to the beautiful messages for life inherent in these teachings find guidelines that bring harmony to one's existence, and joy to life itself.

The woman of the Jewish household is called the עֲקֶרֶת הַבַּיִת, the mainstay of the home, and rightly so. She creates the spiritual environment from which her husband and children benefit. Even before formal Jewish education has begun, she imbues her children with the warmth and beauty that Judaism has to offer. Her meticulous adherence to the *mitzvot* sets the tone for the family, and helps imbue the home with holiness.

This is the beautiful heritage of Judaism. The Torah has been the beacon of light in a long and bitter exile, accompanying Jews from country to country throughout the millennia. The Torah is not merely a historical account of an aged people; it is the eternal testimony to the vibrancy of our nation and our relationship with G-d. We have lived by the Torah and we have died for it, because its *mitzvot* contained lessons that have been handed down from generation to generation.

The Jewish nation's gift to the young woman becoming a Bat Mitzvah is the legacy of our Torah and its traditions. Her gift to her people is the preservation of that cherished heritage through her becoming an important link in the golden chain created by our Matriarchs and other great women in Jewish history.

Role Models for Life

"Who are our role models?" This is a very telling question about what we'd like to do in the future, and how we will shape our lives. To whom does a young girl look for advice and for guidance? Who is the person after whom she will pattern her life? As children we spend most of our lives in the presence of our parents, teachers and friends. Consciously or not, they are teaching — and we are learning. Positive character traits are being shared and, unfortunately, negative ones are also apparent. Do we want to look the way they look? Is our language and the way we talk affected by what we hear from them?

Think for a moment about the media and its idolization of people of fame and fortune. The rich, the talented, the beautiful, the famous people that are in the headlines are certainly people with a high profile. The media will share all the details of their lives, for better or worse, that are of interest to readers and viewers. For a baseball player it may be his athletic exploits, or his fall from grace as he was convicted of substance abuse. When Princess Diana of England was tragically killed in a car accident some years back, interestingly the media focused on some of her activities working with AIDS patients and the disadvantaged. Her prominence and social status were hers since she was born into royalty; her beauty was a gift from the Al-mighty. Her activities on behalf of the disadvantaged were the elements of her life that were the legacy that *everyone* could learn from. We listen to the beautiful voice of a singer — but we may not have that gift. We'll see the talent of an actor, but we may not receive such a Divine present. We can model ourselves after individuals using *our* unique talents, *our* abilities and the "raw materials" that G-d has given us.

The challenges facing a Jewish young lady are diverse and formidable. Developing into a true *bat Yisrael,* daughter of Israel, requires strength of character, the will to excel and, perhaps most of all, vision. The vision that can see the world and grasp its beauty. The vision that can reflect on society and discriminate between truth and deception, virtue and impropriety, and between the practices that promote advancement and those that cause decay.

Fortunately we have our Torah to guide us, the timeless gift of G-d that, through our understanding and utilization, can help shape the lives of all those who seek its meaning and depth. Indeed, the Torah is replete with reminders, imploring us to closely observe the ways of our elders from whose practices and priorities we can glean direction and values for living.

The Jewish woman, throughout our existence, has played a most pivotal role in this generational educational process. Scores of women have displayed a vast array of exemplary characteristics from which so much can be learned. By examining a few of these pioneers of perfection, we can hope to learn from and be inspired by their ways of life.

Our commentators question the grammatical structure of the phrase (משלי יד:א) "חָכְמוֹת נָשִׁים בָּנְתָה בֵיתָהּ" "The wisdom of women built her home" (Proverbs 14:1). Why does the verse begin by using the plural form, women, and then change to the singular, her home? Their answer gives us an insight into the secret of the continuity of the Jewish people.

Any structure is only as strong as its foundation. The taller the building, the more solid its base must be. No lone woman can successfully create the spiritual and emotional climate that is necessary to sustain a Jewish home. She brings the wisdom, the understanding, the insight and the faith that are the legacy of her mother, her grandmother, and countless generations before her. It is these women, with their combined attributes and talents, who are the foundation for the unique home that is built by each one of their descendants. Their treasured legacy is passed on, and another generation carries on the beautiful traditions of Judaism.

Our Sages make an interesting comment about the way we should look at character development. "A person is obliged to say, 'When will my actions reach those of my ancestors?'" Indeed, should every young man fault himself if he falls short of the actions of our Patriarchs? Is every young woman able to replicate the giants of Jewish history and their virtuous deeds, the likes of which haven't been seen for hundreds of years?

In truth, this challenge by our Sages is not exhorting today's young women to accomplish that which earlier generations could not. Perfection is impossible, but it is the responsibility of every individual to seek new ways to better her character and ultimately enrich her lives. If she will always keep the image of earlier great people in her mind, it will inspire her to see what can be accomplished — if she will live up to the potential with which she has been endowed. Our Sages challenge our complacency, urging us to never be satisfied with the mediocre, but always strive for self-actualization. A young woman's reach should exceed her grasp; for if not, what are the heavens for?

Prominent women in Jewish history charted the virtuous courses followed by their descendants through the ages.

In the Merit of Righteous Women

rominent women in Jewish history charted the virtuous courses followed by their descendants through the ages. The women depicted (from right to left) are those introduced in the following section, Role Models in Jewish History.

🐦 🐦 🐦

Sarah was the paragon of modesty, the mainstay of the Jewish home. During her lifetime, the candles were always lit, a blessing was found in the dough, and a cloud was suspended over the tent (*Midrash*).

Rebecca's act of *chesed*, loving kindness was seen by Eliezer when she drew water for him and for his camels, Her deeds made her a fitting mate for Isaac.

Rachel, buried on the way to Beit Lechem, rather than in the Cave of Machpelah, was the source of comfort to the Jews as they were exiled to Babylonia. In the merit of her compassion, we hope to be redeemed one day.

Leah praised G-d for a seemingly natural occurrence, when Yehudah, her fourth son, was born after Reuven, Shimon and Levi.

Batya, the daughter of Pharoah, reached out to the baby Moses in the bulrushes, despite the great distance between them.

Miriam, sister of Moses and Aaron, led the women in joyous song as G-d split the Red Sea for the Jews. The women of that generation anticipated the wondrous salvation of G-d.

Hannah, the childless wife of Elkanah, turned to G-d to grant her the gift of a child. Her lips moved in silent prayer, yet she uttered no audible sound. The High Priest read the message of the breastplate as שִׁכֹּרָה, a drunkard. In truth, the cryptic answer was to be read, כְּשֵׁרָה, virtuous one, or כְּשָׂרָה, like Sarah. The gift to her and to the Jewish people was Samuel the Prophet.

Ruth was steadfastly devoted to her mother-in-law, Naomi, She clung to her, and to the tenets of our faith, and was the great-grandmother of King David, the progenitor of the Davidic dynasty, and, ultimatelty, *Mashiach*.

Queen Esther risked her life by entering the palace of King Achashveirosh, without being summoned. Her self-sacrifice for her people gives Jews through the ages the courage and fortitude to overcome even the most formidable obstacles.

Twelve years ago, a doctor announced excitedly to
anxiously waiting loved ones.
"Congratulations — it's a girl!"
The pure joy of that moment reached beyond the
hearts of your family — it resounded through the
years of Jewish existence: past, present, and future.
A bat Melech, a Jewish daughter to the King,
entered the world with the potential and
opportunity to make a significant, positive
difference touching the lives of those near to her
as well as those far, in a most unique and eloquent
way that only she can do.

How can a Bat Mitzvah make sure she fulfills her
singular role in life? One would have to look at the
crucial midot, qualities, for which the Torah praises
our matriarchs and cultivate them within herself.

How can a
Bat Mitzvah make
sure she fulfills her
singular role in life?

SARAH
שרה

Emunah – The Lifeblood of the Jewish People

Together with her husband, Avraham *Avinu*, Sarah taught the world of the One true G-d, the Creator of the entire universe. Sarah constantly acknowledged the Al-mighty's mastery over all, always seeing His loving hand beneath the surface always. Her diligent focus on the trait of *emunah*, faith, instilled generations of Jewish women with the hope and fortitude that has carried our Nation through the darkest periods of Jewish struggle. The unwavering *emunah* of Jewish women sustained our People through Egyptian slavery, spurred the hastening of our redemption and holds the awesome power to deem us worthy of the final *geulah*, redemption, may it come soon in our days.

This soul-sustaining attribute of *emunah* is crucial when the going gets rough. A Bat Mitzvah can face life's challenges with the faith that Hashem sent them and that each test comes with a vital purpose – always out of love. Not an easy task! the holy efforts of Sarah *Imeinu*, paved the way for every Jewish woman to, not only go through, but *grow* through difficulty.

Every woman can heighten her *emunah* through heartfelt prayer, study, and promoting an awareness of G-d's direct interaction with the world. Women have used their powerful propensity towards *emunah* to strengthen others around them, and even alter the course of Jewish history. While the men despaired under grueling Egyptian oppression, the women demonstrated their faith by effectively and lovingly persuading their husbands to continue to bring Jewish children into the world. When the spies returned with a negative report on the Land of Israel, detailing the threatening forces that would render the Land unconquerable, the men urged that they go back to Egypt. The women, however, were able to see beyond the seemingly bleak odds and understood that if G-d promised the Land to the Jews, no obstacle could stand in their way. *Emunah* – the lifeblood of the Jewish Nation. Each woman possesses this wellspring, giving her the ability to uplift another Jew – including herself – every moment of every day.

REBECCA
רבקה

Chesed –
Holding Up the World

Realizing that the creation of the world and all of life's blessings come from Hashem's limitless desire to give, Abraham and Sarah conscientiously lived G-d's attribute of *chesed*. Every side of their *ohel*, tent, displayed an open door to welcome visitors – offering potent nourishment for the body and soul, any time of night or day.

G-d blessed Sarah's home with three constant miracles. She lit Shabbat candles every Friday night that burned until the following Shabbat eve. Her home-baked *challah* remained fresh throughout the week as well. And a cloud of The Divine Presence continually floated just above her tent. When Sarah left this world the miracles ceased to exist, only to return upon the entrance of Rivka.

When Eliezer, Isaac's servant and matchmaker, traveled to Canaan in search of the proper wife for his master – a person worthy of becoming the next matriarch of the Jewish People – he looked for a young lady of character who actively demonstrated the attribute of kindness. He devised a plan: he stationed himself outside the city near a well at evening – a time when women came to draw. This way he could clearly observe each ones natural behavior, outside her home environment. He then prayed to Hashem for success in his mission and that He make it clear to him which woman had the depth of sensitivity towards others that would prove most appropriate for the stature of Yitzchok's wife and mother to the Jewish Nation.

Hashem responded in the midst of Eliezer's heartfelt petition. Rivka had at that very moment descended from her home towards the well. Eliezer expressed his need for a drink of water and Rivka ran to perform the act of kindness. She lifted her jug towards Eliezer's mouth, sparing him the effort of holding it, and ran back to refill the jugs for his ten thirsty camels until they too were quenched.

Inherent in every Jewish woman lies the potential to perceive the needs of others and the ability to graciously fulfill them in her own inimitable way. All it takes is a desire to help and the opportunities for acts of *chesed* become very clear. There's a friend who needs words of encouragement, someone ailing in the hospital who would delight in a friendly visitor, a lonely elderly neighbor who could use some uplifting company, a busy mother (perhaps yours) who needs a helping hand in the house…

What a difference YOU can make!

Rachel
רחל

The Poweʀ op Modesty and Selp-Sacʀipice

A person's choices reveal and serve to create his/her character – especially during times of great difficulty. Our Matriarch, Rachel, faced a monumental challenge and the tremendous effort behind her decision both revealed and actualized her greatness. Her courage and extraordinary modesty held the power to bring the Jewish People's ultimate redemption.

For seven years she waited to marry her intended, Yaakov. Rightfully suspicious of her deceitful father, Laban, Rachel feared that, on their wedding day, he would send Leah, her older sister, to Yaakov in her stead. Rachel and Yaakov exchanged a series of identifying passwords so that Yaakov would know beyond a doubt that it was Rachel he had taken to be his wife. At the moment of the anticipated switch, Rachel's heart went out to her sister. Motivated by profound compassion, she decided to suppress her own desire and sacrifice her long awaited opportunity for marriage to Yaakov. Sharing the secret signals with Leah, she spared her sister from dreadful humiliation.

The *Midrash* records that at the time of the Temple's destruction and Israel's bitter exile, each of the Patriarchs pleaded with Hashem to show compassion on His People. In order to stir G-d's mercy, each related the suffering he had endured and invoked his individual merit. Hashem remained, as it were, unmoved. Rachel stepped forward. "I performed an act of kindness for my sister, Leah. I was not jealous of her, and did not expose her shame. I, who am flesh and blood, dust and ashes whose nature it is to be jealous ... You, O Eternal, Merciful King – why were You jealous of idolatry, which has no substance? Why did You exile my children and let the enemies slaughter them...?" Rachel's words aroused Hashem's compassion. "For Rachel I will return the people of Israel to their place" (*Pesikta Eichah Rabbati* 24).

Rachel stretched beyond human nature to spare a fellow Jew's feelings and created the powerful potential for self-sacrifice and modesty in all future generations of Jewish women. You too can make difficult choices in order to protect another. Refraining from speaking negatively about another Jew can save him or her from disfavor and emotional hurt, save you from a serious transgression, and save the Jewish People from harm. And while you're choosing – you're creating a better you.

Leah לאה

Gratitude – At the Root of Judaism

The gossipers of the time set about doing their own matchmaking. "Isaac has two sons, Esav and Yaakov. Lavan has two daughters, Leah and Rachel. The older son, Esav, will marry the older daughter, Leah, and the younger son, Yaakov, will wed the younger daughter, Rachel!" Upon learning of Esav's evil character, Leah wept and prayed that Hashem free her from the edict and not "fall to the lot of a wicked man." G-d responded to her relentless tears and in fact she preceded her sister in marrying the righteous Yaakov. It wasn't smooth sailing from there, either. People jeered at her, saying, "This Leah is not inwardly as she appears. If she were righteous, she would not have deceived her sister" (*Bereishis Rabbah* 71:2). Nonetheless, Leah persevered as the mother of the Jewish Nation, a privilege she worked tirelessly to achieve. She valued each blessing.

The Sages of the *Midrash* made a statement that requires reflection: "There was no person who praised G-d until Leah came along." A most perplexing declaration. Surely our sacred patriarchs, Abraham and Isaac, praised G-d for the miracles that they witnessed and from which they reaped benefit. They even brought sacrifices of appreciation to Hashem. Then why does the Talmud record that no one prior to Leah even praised G-d?

The *K'tav Sofer* offers an enlightening explanation, teaching us a powerful lesson. When Leah gave birth to her fourth son, Judah, she declared, "This time let me gratefully praise Hashem" (*Bereishis* 29:25). True, others acknowledged G-d's greatness before Leah did, but only in response to miracles. The birth of a child, while clearly an incredible phenomenon, is still an everyday occurrence. Leah cultivated the insight to perceive G-d's miraculous ways even within the natural order of things. It was this exceptional characteristic that prompted our Sages to proclaim her as the first to truly praise Hashem.

How many of us take the time to stop and think of the blessings G-d grants us each day? Yet, it feels so natural to notice what's missing in our lives. Try a truly eye-opening exercise each night before you go to sleep. Make a mental or written list of virtually everything you are grateful to have. Keep this up and gratitude will just flow naturally. After all, a rich person is one who is happy with whatever he or she has. One cannot be happy with what one has until he or she does a complete conscious inventory – and then, like our mother, Leah, expresses a heartfelt "Thank you!"

BATYA
בתיה

Inspiring Help from Above

The compassion of Batya, daughter of Pharaoh, was awakened by the poignant cries of baby Moshe, as he lay in a basket floating down the Nile. Although the task seemed – and was – in fact naturally impossible, she promptly reached out her arm to save him. Hashem responded to Batya's *chesed* and *hishtadlut*, effort, by supernaturally extending her arm so that she could succeed in her effort to rescue him.

Batya, a little-known figure in Jewish history, maintains a position of prominence because of her essential role as the one who saved Moshe from the Nile Her name is not even mentioned in the Torah; she is merely referred to as *bat* Pharoah, the daughter of the Pharoah. Even in *Chronicles* I, 4:18, she is called Bitya, rather than Batya! Her stature was great in that she was the daughter of Pharoah, but her name Batya means "daughter of G-d."

The *Midrash*, the narrative portion of the Oral Torah, sheds light on Batya's character. The handmaidens that came with her challenged her decision to save the Jewish baby. "In the normal manner of the world," they said, "the king makes a decision and nonetheless there are still some subjects who disregard it. *Your father*, the Pharoah, decreed that all Jewish babies should be thrown into the Nile, and you are defying that decree!" The *Midrash* relates that the angel Gabriel came and killed them all to allow the saving of Moses. Imagine the courage it must have taken to go against the orders of her own father, the king, to do what was right! Batya brought Moshe back to the palace and raised the savior of the Jewish nation.

The Talmud (*Megillah* 13a) relates that after helping shape the destiny of the Jewish people, Batya married Mered, another name for Caleb, one of the two spies who brought back a favorable report about Israel when sent by Moses. *Mered* means to rebel. "Let Caleb, who rebelled against the plan of the spies, marry Batya, who rebelled against the idolatry of her father's house." The strength of character that Batya possessed deemed her a worthy life partner for the leader who helped us conquer the land of Israel.

If each of us "reached out" to help those in need in our community – even though we feel our efforts won't make a difference – each time we try, we could be inspiring compassion from Above and Divine assistance to help us succeed. Our job is to respond, like Batya, by making the active effort, and trust that G-d will do the rest.

MIRIAM

מִרְיָם

Learning from Miriam's Holy Courage

When life around us runs smoothly – the days are sunny, the family is healthy, you aced your social studies exam, and summer vacation is around the corner – then we readily accept G-d's benevolence. Unless we work constantly on this essential Jewish belief with a deep-rooted trust and conviction, however, during troubled times we can easily lose our faith in Hashem's infinite goodness.

Miriam the prophetess, sister to Moshe *Rabbeinu*, exemplified unwavering faith in the face of a seemingly hopeless situation. Pharaoh decreed that every Jewish family throw all newborn males into the Nile River . Her father, Amram, decided it was wise to separate from his wife, Yocheved, to avoid confronting such a horrifying position. Miriam's impenetrable trust in Hashem's grand design for the Jewish Nation motivated her to draw from her wellspring of spiritual courage and convince her parents to reunite. They did, and Moshe *Rabbeinu*, Hashem's chosen leader who brought the Torah to the Jewish Nation, was born.

Shifrah (Yocheved) and Puah (Miriam) served as the Hebrew midwives during the oppressive Egyptian enslavement. They defied Pharaoh's orders to kill all the male Jewish babies, and, in fact, did everything in their power to assist the Jewish women in childbirth. They also lovingly cared for their infants after delivery. Because of a mother and daughter's tenacity of faith, seeing themselves as tools in the service of Hashem, the Jewish People survived and flourished.

The faith and trust that Miriam exhibited was not only evident as a young girl when she helped save her brother. The Jews were promised that they would be redeemed, and hoped against hope that their salvation would soon take place. Miriam and the women turned their hope into action. They didn't wait for the actual miracle of the splitting of the sea to take place. With drums and cymbals readied, Miriam anticipated the redemption as soon as they were told it would occur. Such was the exalted bearing of the women of that generation. Confident in G-d's promise that He would save the Jewish nation from the Egyptians, the instruments to thank G-d were taken out with them.

Every Jewish woman carries an optimistic heart – beating with trust and conviction in Hashem's benevolent plan for the Jewish People and for each individual Jew. Like Miriam, we possess the ability to see a better tomorrow, and to influence others to persevere in their hope. See what happens through a single woman's efforts! We too – each Jewish woman – can help move the course of time toward our ultimate redemption.

NAOMI and RUTH
נָעֳמִי וְרוּת

Ruth and Naomi –
Devotion Assures Jewish Eternity

During the period of the Judges, Israel had no king to properly lead them, and many Jews strayed from the path of the Torah. Hashem then brought a famine to the Land. Elimelech, the leader of the generation, left Israel's spiritually and economically impoverished population behind and settled in the prosperous land of Moab with his wife, Naomi, and their two sons. His sons later intermarried with Orpah and Ruth, two daughters of the Moabite king, Eglon. Elimelech died in Moab, followed by his two sons, leaving Naomi and her two daughters-in-law impoverished widows.

Throughout her stay in Moab, Naomi had longed to go back to the land of her People. With her husband and sons gone, she decided to return. She assured her daughters-in-law that she would manage fine without them; they could remain in Moab. Ruth refused to leave her side, insisting, "Wherever you go, I will go. Your people are my people. And your G-d is my G-d." Although Ruth came from the uncompassionate people of Moab, but despite her ancestry, she demonstrated genuine kindness, compassion, and appreciation towards her mother-in-law. Through her steadfast devotion to the Jewish People, she merited becoming a "mother of royalty" and lived until the reign of her great-great-grandson, King Solomon.

Orpah and Ruth faced a formidable challenge and each chose her consequential reaction. Our Sages characterize them as "The one who kissed (Naomi) and left, Orpah, and the one who clung tenaciously to her," a reference to Ruth. This dedicated convert to Judaism realized that she could never leave her widowed mother-in-law, and she remained a lifelong support for her. Orpah returned to Moab, completely severed the bond with Naomi, and eventually became the mother of Goliath, antagonist of (King) David. Two women made individual decisions that dramatically affected their lives and the destiny of our people.

The image of Ruth the convert, clinging to her broken yet beloved mother-in-law, teaches us an eternal lesson in dedication, commitment, and in the primacy of familial preservation and support. Boaz saw Ruth's exemplary character and G-d chose them to be the progenitors of the Davidic Kingdom. An individual that exemplifies such unswerving dedication is worthy of being the mother of our nation, enabling us to be faithful servants in the pursuit of all 613 *mitzvot*.

chana
חנה

To Speak to the Almighty –
An Awesome Privilege

Think about it. The Creator of the Universe wants to hear from you every day. You can present any need or longing – no matter how seemingly "small" or "large" – to the One Who can do absolutely anything, anywhere, anytime, without obstacle. And the Receiver of your requests loves you with a love stronger than you can comprehend. All that is required is thorough concentration as you direct your voice and your heart to Hashem – Who waits patiently for your pleading whispers.

Chana, wife of Elkanah, knew well of the life-changing power of prayer, and pursued it wisely and fervently; so much so that many of the laws connected with how we recite the *shemonah esrei*, the central prayer in the *siddur*, come directly from the manner in which Chana prayed for a child. Chana longed to bear children and prayed arduously for 20 years. One Rosh Hashanah she went to the Holy Temple and stood before her Creator, and through her heartfelt tears, she silently moved her lips as she prayed. To this day we all pray the *shemonah esrei* according to Chana's example.

Chana concluded her prayer with the promise that if G-d would grant her a child, she would dedicate him to serve Him in the Temple. Chana soon thereafter gave birth to a baby boy, Shmuel, the prophet. And Chana kept her promise.

The Torah reading on Rosh Hashanah speaks of G-d remembering the barren Sarah and granting her a child. The *Haftarah* describes Chana's heartfelt pleas for a child. The Talmud (*Megillah* 31a) tells us that both women were remembered on that day – Rosh Hashanah, the Day of Remembrance, when we call out to G-d and proclaim Him as King. Just as Chana beseeched G-d in sincere prayer — and was answered — we come before Him with *our* own fervent pleas, for a year of health and happiness.

Chana taught us how to pray, and how effective sincere words of prayer can be. To pray with *kavanah*, full concentration, requires the belief that G-d is listening to every word and every sigh, to believe that He cares deeply, and will answer – according to *His* time frame. For only Hashem knows what is best for us and the right moment to deliver the *berachot*. That's why they are called blessings. What better time to receive a gift than when we are ready to fully appreciate it? His line is always open. No call waiting, no appointments! And He really wants to hear from you, today and forever.

ESTHER אסתר

The Courage of Esther

On the 13th of Adar each year, children gleefully dress up in costume and Jews everywhere fulfill the *mitzvot* of exchanging gifts with their friends and making certain to provide for the poor. Purim represents the happiest of days and we will continue to celebrate its advent even after our long-awaited redemption. Upon the strength of one woman's bravery, Hashem saved the Jewish People from Haman's malicious plans.

When Esther agreed to go to King Achashveirosh, she did so at the risk of her life. As she journeyed to the king, she poured her heart out to Hashem. The *Midrash* says that Esther went down a long corridor, into the courtyard of the "the king" – *HaMelech*. We know that whenever the *Megillat* Esther reads "the *Melech*", it refers, on a deeper level, to Hashem, the King of all kings. Esther was going to the *Kodesh HaKadoshim,* the Holy of Holies. That was her goal, to reach Hashem in the most private of places, to talk with the King, to plead for the Jewish People.

Although forbidden to approach the king uninvited, Esther proceeded with confidence and immersed herself with prayer. Through her tefilla, opening herself up so completely to G-d for the sake of *Klal Yisrael*, she moved beyond her fears and rose to a level of actually working in tandem with Hashem. Saving the Jewish People became her only concern.

Achashveirosh pointed his scepter and asked, "What is it that you want, Esther?" She began to implement her plans of action, and the rest, as they say, is Jewish history. Esther realized that Hashem had placed her in the role of queen so that she could choose to take the responsibility to help save her brethren, and at the risk of her life, she inspired miracles.

Like Esther, Hashem gave each one of us our unique station in life, where, with courage and trust in G-d's help, we can also inspire miracles.

A Woman of Valor

who can find? Far beyond pearls is her worth. Her husband's heart trusts in her and he shall lack no fortune. She repays his good but never his harm, all the days of her life. She seeks out wool and flax and her hands work willingly. She was like the merchant's ships. From afar she brings her bread. From sleep she arises while it is still night, to give food to her household and what is due to her maidens. She thinks of a field and buys it. From the fruits of her labor she planted a vineyard. With might she girded her loins and strengthened her arms. She feels that her venture is good, her lamp is not snuffed out at night, her hand reaches out for the distaff, and her palms support the spindle. She extends her palm to the poor and sends her hand out to the destitute. She fears not snow for her household, for her household is attired in scarlet wool. Fine carpets she made for herself, of linen and purple wool is her clothing. Well known in the councils is her husband, when he sits among the elders. Strength and splendor are her clothing, and she awaits with joy the very last day. Her mouth she opens with wisdom and the lesson of lovingkindness is on her tongue. She keeps watch over the ways her household and eats not of the bread of laziness. Her children arise and praise her; her husband, and he lauds her. Many are the daughters who have achieved valor, but you surpassed them all. Charm is false and beauty is futile, a woman who fears Hashem, she should be praised. Give to her from the fruits of her labor and let her be praised in the gates by her very own deeds.

AYSHET CHA-YIL mi yimtzo, v'rochōk mip'ninim michroh. Botach boh layv baloh, v'sholol lō yechsor. G'molat-hu tōv v'lō ro, kōl y'may cha-yeho. Dor'sho tzemer ufishtim, vata-as b'chayfetz kapeho. Hoy'to ko-oniyōt sōchayr, mimerchok tovi lachmoh. Vatokom b'ōd lailoh, vatitayn teref l'vaytah, v'chōk l'na-arōteho. Zom'mo sode vatikochayhu, mip'ri chapeho not'o korem. Chog'roh b'ōz motneho, vat'amaytz z'rō-ōteho. To-amo ki tōv sachroh, lō yichbe balailo nayroh. Yodeho shil'cho vakishōr, v'chapeho tom'chu folech. Kapoh por'so le-oni, v'yodeho shil'cho lo-evyôn. Lō tiro l'vaytah misholeg, ki chol baytah lovush shonim. Marvadim os'ta loh, shaysh v'argomon l'vushoh. Nōdo bash'orim baloh, b'shivtō im ziknay oretz. Sodin os'ta vatimkōr, vachagōr not'no lak'na-ani. Ōz v'hodor l'vushoh, vatis-chak l'yōm acharōn. Piho pot'cho v'chochmo, v'tōras chesed al l'shōnoh. Tzōfiyoh halichōt baytah, v'lechem atzlut lō tōchayl. Komu voneho vai-ash'ruho, baloh vai-hal'loh. Rabōt banōt osu cho-yil, v'at olit al kulono. Sheker hachayn v'hevel hayōfi, isho yir-at Adōnoy hi tit-halol. T'nu loh mip'ri yodeho, vihal'luho vash'orim ma-aseho.

אֵשֶׁת חַיִל

אֵשֶׁת חַיִל מִי יִמְצָא וְרָחֹק מִפְּנִינִים מִכְרָהּ:

בָּטַח בָּהּ לֵב בַּעְלָהּ וְשָׁלָל לֹא יֶחְסָר:

גְּמָלַתְהוּ טוֹב וְלֹא רָע כֹּל יְמֵי חַיֶּיהָ:

דָּרְשָׁה צֶמֶר וּפִשְׁתִּים וַתַּעַשׂ בְּחֵפֶץ כַּפֶּיהָ:

הָיְתָה כָּאֳנִיּוֹת סוֹחֵר מִמֶּרְחָק תָּבִיא לַחְמָהּ:

וַתָּקָם בְּעוֹד לַיְלָה וַתִּתֵּן טֶרֶף לְבֵיתָהּ וְחֹק לְנַעֲרֹתֶיהָ:

זָמְמָה שָׂדֶה וַתִּקָּחֵהוּ מִפְּרִי כַפֶּיהָ נָטְעָה כָּרֶם:

חָגְרָה בְעוֹז מָתְנֶיהָ וַתְּאַמֵּץ זְרוֹעֹתֶיהָ:

טָעֲמָה כִּי טוֹב סַחְרָהּ לֹא יִכְבֶּה בַלַּיְלָה נֵרָהּ:

יָדֶיהָ שִׁלְּחָה בַכִּישׁוֹר וְכַפֶּיהָ תָּמְכוּ פָלֶךְ:

כַּפָּהּ פָּרְשָׂה לֶעָנִי וְיָדֶיהָ שִׁלְּחָה לָאֶבְיוֹן:

לֹא תִירָא לְבֵיתָהּ מִשָּׁלֶג כִּי כָל בֵּיתָהּ לָבֻשׁ שָׁנִים:

מַרְבַדִּים עָשְׂתָה לָּהּ שֵׁשׁ וְאַרְגָּמָן לְבוּשָׁהּ:

נוֹדָע בַּשְּׁעָרִים בַּעְלָהּ בְּשִׁבְתּוֹ עִם זִקְנֵי אָרֶץ:

סָדִין עָשְׂתָה וַתִּמְכֹּר וַחֲגוֹר נָתְנָה לַכְּנַעֲנִי:

עֹז וְהָדָר לְבוּשָׁהּ וַתִּשְׂחַק לְיוֹם אַחֲרוֹן:

פִּיהָ פָּתְחָה בְחָכְמָה וְתוֹרַת חֶסֶד עַל לְשׁוֹנָהּ:

צוֹפִיָּה הֲלִיכוֹת בֵּיתָהּ וְלֶחֶם עַצְלוּת לֹא תֹאכֵל:

קָמוּ בָנֶיהָ וַיְאַשְּׁרוּהָ בַּעְלָהּ וַיְהַלְלָהּ:

רַבּוֹת בָּנוֹת עָשׂוּ חָיִל וְאַתְּ עָלִית עַל כֻּלָּנָה:

שֶׁקֶר הַחֵן וְהֶבֶל הַיֹּפִי אִשָּׁה יִרְאַת יְיָ הִיא תִתְהַלָּל:

תְּנוּ לָהּ מִפְּרִי יָדֶיהָ וִיהַלְלוּהָ בַשְּׁעָרִים מַעֲשֶׂיהָ:

Building Character:

Perfecting
Our Midot

Reb Yisrael Salanter

he Thirteen *Midot*, or Principles for Life are attributed to Rabbi Yisrael Lipkin, known as Reb Yisrael Salanter (1810-1883). Reb Yisrael is said to be the father of the *mussar* movement, which espoused Torah-guided ethical behavior. Reb Yisrael, a student of Rabbi Zundel of Salant, hoped to rejuvenate traditional Jewry by deepening religious commitment based on a strong initial ethical and behavioral foundation. The *Haskalah*, or "enlightenment" movement had eroded some of the support of normative Judaism, and had deviated from the traditional practices of our faith. In many respects, *mussar* was an attempt to infuse the Jews with a commitment to personal character development and a principled way of life.

Reb Yisrael was a great scholar, teacher and thinker. Based on classical texts such as *Mesillat Yesharim*, Path of the Just by Rav Moshe Chaim Luzzato, he helped formulate the Mussar Movement. Lectures and publications helped establish the philosophy of Reb Yisrael, where *mussar* would be infused into every aspect of Jewish life and practice.

A profound Torah personality is one who has integrated the teachings of *mussar* into his basic character. In the non-Torah world, heads of state can be accused of behavior which is neither ethical, or moral, as leadership abilities don't always go hand in hand with virtue. The teachings of *mussar*, which have laid the foundation for the traditional institute of higher learning, help create a better person, a better Jew and a better world.

The cardinal directions for living have been succinctly encapsulated by Reb Yisrael Salanter into thirteen traits and their explanations. The author has added various statements and teachings from the Talmud and commentaries to highlight the concepts Reb Yisrael espoused.

In many respects, mussar was an attempt to infuse the Jews with a commitment to personal character development and a principled way of life.

THE THIRTEEN MIDOS of REB YISRAEL SALANTER

הנהגות החיים על פי מדות
ר' ישראל סאלאנטער

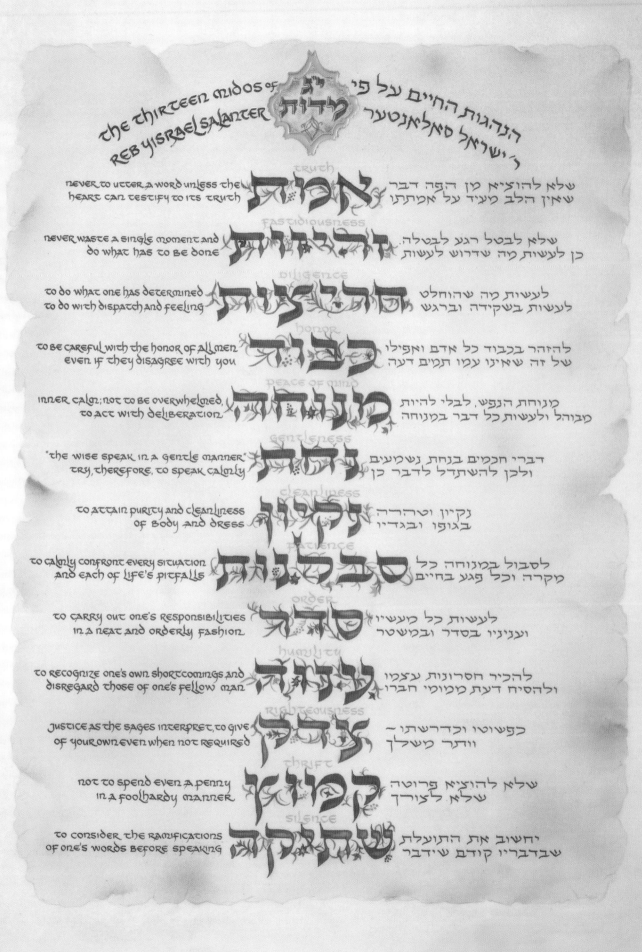

TRUTH — אמת
NEVER TO UTTER A WORD UNLESS THE HEART CAN TESTIFY TO ITS TRUTH
שלא להוציא מן הפה דבר שאין הלב מעיד על אמתתו

FASTIDIOUSNESS — זהירות
NEVER WASTE A SINGLE MOMENT AND DO WHAT HAS TO BE DONE
שלא לבטל רגע לבטלה. כן לעשות מה שדרוש לעשות

DILIGENCE — חריצות
TO DO WHAT ONE HAS DETERMINED TO DO WITH DISPATCH AND FEELING
לעשות מה שהוחלט לעשות בשקידה וברגש

HONOR — כבוד
TO BE CAREFUL WITH THE HONOR OF ALL MEN EVEN IF THEY DISAGREE WITH YOU
להזהר בכבוד כל אדם ואפילו של זה שאינו עמו תמים דעה

PEACE OF MIND — מנוחה
INNER CALM; NOT TO BE OVERWHELMED, TO ACT WITH DELIBERATION
מנוחת הנפש, לבלי להיות מבוהל ולעשות כל דבר במנוחה

GENTLENESS — נחת
"THE WISE SPEAK IN A GENTLE MANNER" TRY, THEREFORE, TO SPEAK CALMLY
דברי חכמים בנחת נשמעים ולכן להשתדל לדבר כן

CLEANLINESS — נקיון
TO ATTAIN PURITY AND CLEANLINESS OF BODY AND DRESS
נקיון וטהרה בגופו ובגדיו

PATIENCE — סבלנות
TO CALMLY CONFRONT EVERY SITUATION AND EACH OF LIFE'S PITFALLS
לסבול במנוחה כל מקרה וכל פגע בחיים

ORDER — סדר
TO CARRY OUT ONE'S RESPONSIBILITIES IN A NEAT AND ORDERLY FASHION
לעשות כל מעשיו ועניניו בסדר ובמשטר

HUMILITY — ענוה
TO RECOGNIZE ONE'S OWN SHORTCOMINGS AND DISREGARD THOSE OF ONE'S FELLOW MAN
להכיר חסרונות עצמו ולהסיח דעת ממומי חברו

RIGHTEOUSNESS — צדק
JUSTICE AS THE SAGES INTERPRET, TO GIVE OF YOUR OWN EVEN WHEN NOT REQUIRED
כפשוטו וכדרשתו וותר משלך

THRIFT — קמוץ
NOT TO SPEND EVEN A PENNY IN A FOOLHARDY MANNER
שלא להוציא פרוטה שלא לצורך

SILENCE — שתיקה
TO CONSIDER THE RAMIFICATIONS OF ONE'S WORDS BEFORE SPEAKING
יחשוב את התועלת שבדבריו קודם שידבר

אמת
Truth

Never to utter a word unless the heart can testify to the truth.

"The signet ring, the divine seal of the Holy One, Blessed be He, is truth" (Talmud, *Shabbat* 55a). Why is truth so important that it is synonymous with the signature of the Almighty? There is only one G-d, and that means that anything else is a false god. So it is with truth. Truth in its purest form is absolute, and even something which is 99% true has a degree of falsehood in it. The unity of truth says that anything else is really false.

Reb Yisrael Salanter's definition about the heart testifying to a truth is puzzling. Doesn't one *speak* the truth rather than *think* it? The story in the Talmud (*Makkot* 24a) illustrates this point.

Rav Safra had an item to sell. A prosperous buyer approached him, offering a sum of money for the object. Rav Safra didn't acknowledge the offer, as he was reciting *kriat shema*. Unaware of the reason for the silence, the buyer raised his offer, only to be met by the same response. He again raised his bid, thinking that Rav Safra rejected the offer because it was insignificant. When Rav Safra finished the *shema*, he accepted the initial amount offered by the buyer. "In my heart, I had acquiesced to the amount, but couldn't reveal my wishes because I was reciting the *shema*." Rav Safra exemplified the phrase דֹּבֵר אֱמֶת בִּלְבָבוֹ (תהלים טו:ב), and he speaks truth in his heart (*Psalms* 15:2).

"The tongue is the quill of the heart" (Duties of the Heart). To be totally truthful, one's speech and actions should actually reflect the thoughts of his heart. If one trains his thoughts to be truthful, he will eventually be in total control of himself, speaking and acting in a Torah-true manner.

זריזות
Fastidiousness

Never waste a single moment and do what has to be done.

In life, there are people that do, and there are *doers*. In Judaism, our Sages place a high priority on the precious gift of time we have been granted by the A-lmighty. If one recognizes that life is precious, every minute is dear, he will live life with a tremendous sense of urgency.

"There's so much I have to do in life!" one should think. The Rabbis see time, particularly in the area of Torah study and the performance of *mitzvot*, as a very precious commodity. "If you forsake Me for a day, I will forsake you for two" (*Sifrei, Parshat Eikev* 11:22). If one doesn't take advantage of the many growth-oriented opportunities that life has, he doesn't remain stagnant; he will in fact be moving backward. One who has taken a train in the wrong direction, must first get back to the original starting point before embarking on his intended destination. By not moving forward, by wasting valuable time, we move further away from where we need to be.

Reb Yisrael Salanter's second comment about זְרִיזוּת, fastidiousness, gives us another component of what that character trait entails. *Doing what has to be done* means being prepared to overcome all obstacles to accomplish your goals. Just as one wouldn't take a trip for a vacation without carefully planning out an itinerary, so it is with all we do in life. "Who is wise — he who sees what will transpire" (Talmud, *Tamid* 32). By advance planning, preparation and an eye towards the future, we have created a blueprint for success in life.

> *On the day of his eldest son's Bar Mitzvah, Rav Yaakov Kamenetsky* זצ"ל *(1891-1986) called this new member of the Jewish nation into his study. "I wish to give you a gift that befits a person of your newly assumed stature. Cherish it and use it wisely." His son carefully unwrapped the package and admired his new wristwatch. Rav Yaakov shared the message of his gift. "Reb Yisrael Salanter would say that time is life; if one is careful with his time, he has actually lost out on the time to accomplish great things.*

To do what one has determined to do with dispatch and feeling.

Look around at many successful people in life. What are some of the qualities that make them stand out from their counterparts? Is it their intellect? Their talents? Their background? You might find that what sets them apart is their diligence, a concentrated, focused energy on working towards one's goals. An industrious individual isn't just hard-working; he's willing to pursue his goal and not let outside interference stand in the way of reaching it. Imagine trying to select a favorite radio program at night, only to hear the static of another station disrupting your reception. Once you've "locked in" to the station you desire, all the other static is disregarded and your station will be heard.

In addition to *what* you'll be doing, one should look at *how* you'll be doing it. "... *this nation has honored Me with its mouth and its lips, but its heart is far from Me, and its fear of Me is like men observing the commandments by rote" (Isaiah 29:13).* We can do an action because we've grown accustomed to doing it, or we can put our hearts and feelings into it. Certain actions have to be done because they are part of life (like cleaning up our room!). Our attitude towards the action elevates it from being a bothersome chore to becoming a significant activity which fulfills the will of our Creator. If you set your heart and mind to invigorating your actions, you can accomplish great things in life.

In Torah study, one who is diligent is called a *matmid* from the root word *tamid*, or constant. This doesn't only mean that he will invest long hours to be immersed in his studies, certainly a necessary quality to be a *matmid*. One who spends much time in the study hall, but uses only half of it for actual study, does not deserve this special title. The qualitative use of his time, spending almost 60 minutes of every hour in study, enables the *matmid* to gracefully wear the title he so deserves.

כבוד
Honor

To be careful with the honor of all men even if they disagree with you.

In Judaism, there are so many different types of honor and respect. There is כְּבוֹד שָׁמַיִם, the honor of Heaven, performing actions which will bring honor to G-d's Name. In our human interactions, there are also many different types of honor. There is כָּבוֹד הוֹרִים, honor of one's parents, כָּבוֹד חֲבֵרִים, honoring one's friends, and כָּבוֹד הַבְּרִיּוֹת, the basic honor for any individual.

What do our Sages tell us about what it takes to be an honorable person?

אֵיזֶהוּ מְכֻבָּד הַמְכַבֵּד אֶת הַבְּרִיּוֹת שֶׁנֶּאֱמַר.
כִּי־מְכַבְּדַי אֲכַבֵּד וּבֹזַי יֵקַלּוּ (שמואל א' ב:ל)

"Who is worthy of honor? He who honors his fellow man, as it is said, 'Those who honor Me, I will honor, and those who despise Me will be held in contempt' (Samuel I 2:30)"
[*Pirkei Avot*, Chapter 4:1].

The *mishnah* discusses an honorable person, yet quotes a verse which extols the value of one who honors G-d. How do we reconcile this apparent inconsistency between the statement and the corroborating verse? In truth, any honor to a person stems from our recognition that he was created in the image of G-d. The spark of Divinity that rests in every human being is truly worthy of honor, and by honoring another human being, we bring honor to He who created him.

וְאָהַבְתָּ לְרֵעֲךָ כָּמוֹךָ אֲנִי ה' (ויקרא יט:יח)
"Love your fellow man as yourself – I am Hashem
(*Leviticus 19:18*).

The Torah's statement about loving one's friend indicates why it is such a fundamentally important *mitzvah*. The closing statement in the verse, "I am your G-d," is in effect the reason for the first half. One must love his fellow man, whether he is of like mind or not, because it was G-d Who created us all (*R' Dovid Kronglas*).

Inner calm; never to be overwhelmed, to act with deliberatio

Every single day a battle is being waged inside each and every one of us. We are comprised of the גוּף, our physical essence, and the נְשָׁמָה, our spiritual self. The body pulls us in the direction which may be momentarily satisfying, but ultimately in conflict with the needs of the soul. The tension that results will put the individual in a state of uneasiness, and the inner peace and harmony that he seeks will elude him. In truth, the struggle can ultimately be a positive experience, if it spurs the individual on to a pattern of growth. Whether it's in the realm of *mitzvah* observance or character development, we can be a better person today than we were yesterday.

The inner calm that every person seeks, the sense of contentment that so few people in our fast-paced, technologically challenging society possess, is a prize worth pursuing. As discussed in the character trait of זְרִיזוּת, fastidiousness, a sense of direction, knowing where you are headed at the outset, is extremely beneficial. The body and soul reach a state of mutual coexistence as they work together to purposefully pursue the goals they have set forth.

In Judaism, we are given a weekly opportunity to find that much-needed מְנוּחָה, peace of mind. Shabbat is referred to as a day of contentment. The soul is refreshed and the body enjoys physical enjoyment in a spiritual context. *Pele Yoetz* (Rabbi Eliezer Papo, 1785-1828) suggests that one's ultimate goal of inner harmony should be directed towards עוֹלָם הַבָּא, the World to Come. At that time, when each man and woman, and the totality of mankind, will reach the pinnacle of spiritual perfection, body and soul will fuse to invest it with a more elevated sense of self.

The Merciful One, may He bequeath us a day of Shabbat and contentment. This phrase, added to the Grace After Meals on Shabbat, is a reference to the day of ultimate Shabbat — the World to Come. One strives on this world with the help of Shabbat, a semblance of the World to Come, to reach a state of contentment and peace.

נחת
Gentleness

The wise speak in a gentle manner;
try, therefore to speak calmly.

While peace of mind, מְנוּחָה, is the ultimate goal of our actions, consciously speaking in a refined and gentle manner helps us achieve our goal. When we are angry inside, even if at times it seems totally justified, we lose focus. "One who gets angry is considered as if he worshipped idols!" (*Zohar Chadash* 58a). "Idols??!" you exclaim. "I know I lost my cool; but how can you possibly say I worshipped idols!!"

Rambam (*Hilchot Dei'ot* 2:3) says that although someone should generally take a middle-of-the-road stance regarding most character traits, there are two which he should avoid to the extreme: conceit and anger. In fact, there is a common thread between them. We are given talents and abilities by G-d, but sometimes we take credit for things which we could never accomplish without His help. Of course, we can feel proud if we achieve, because we are supposed to feel good about ourselves. Conceit, however, denies the element of G-d's involvement in our accomplishments. The "false god" that we are worshipping is ourselves!

When we get angry, we fall into the grips of another false god. We completely lose control of ourselves, and sometimes will do things that simply don't make sense. We move away from where G-d wants us to be, and our anger takes over.

"Judges and officers you shall place in all your gates" (*Deuteronomy* 16:18). Where are these gates? *Shelah* explains that they are the openings in our body – our mouth, and our ears – and we must guard them carefully. We have to make sure that things we shouldn't say don't exit our lips, and things we shouldn't hear don't enter our ears. Even if we feel anger in our hearts, we are given another safeguard to make sure it doesn't express itself in a way that is not appropriate. If we speak calmly, eventually we can even control the anger in our heart, and achieve the peace we are seeking.

Attaining Purity of Body and Dress

As Jews, we serve as G-d's ambassadors on earth. In the *shema*, we say, "You should love G-d with all your heart and all your soul and all your resources." The Talmud (*Yoma* 86a) explains that loving G-d also means causing G-d to be beloved. When people in the street see us looking neat and well groomed in appropriate dress, when they observe us dealing and speaking pleasantly with people, they'll say, "Fortunate is he whose father taught him Torah, fortunately is he whose teacher taught him Torah!" Our actions reflect not only upon ourselves, but also on our parents, our teachers and on G-d Himself. If a child dresses in soiled clothing, it reflects poorly on his parents; if *we* dress in soiled clothing, it reflects the level of G-dliness that we maintain.

Carefully tending to the cleanliness of the body, our bodily needs, and guarding one's health are all included in a Torah directive and carry *halachic* ramifications. "And you shall greatly beware for your souls" (*Deuteronomy* 4:15). Proper hygiene is important as well as a *mitzvah*. One must have the proper physical state of readiness before engaging in prayer before the Creator.

Mesilat Yesharim, the classic work by Rabbi Moshe Chaim Luzzato, provides a comprehensive guide for character perfection and adds another dimension to the purity towards which one should strive. One might be careful to safeguard his or her actions, but still may not be *pure* in his intentions. If we carefully weigh our actions before we do them, people who see us will view what we do favorably. Our actions should find favor in the eyes of G-d and of man.

Based on the statement in the Talmud, (*Avodah Zarah* 20a) *Mesilat Yesharim* lists cleanliness on an ascending list of positive character traits. "Torah leads to watchfulness, watchfulness leads to zeal, zeal leads to cleanliness, cleanliness leads to separation, separation leads to purity, purity leads to saintliness, saintliness leads to humility, etc." As a crucial, foundational character trait, cleanliness of body, dress and mind creates a steppingstone to help a Jew achieve great things.

סבלנות
Patience

To calmly confront every situation and each of life's pitfalls.

How good and how pleasant is patience; this character trait is needed by every person! (*Pele Yoetz*). A communal leader faces instances where his patience is tested by his constituents. A spouse, parent or teacher is faced with infinite opportunities to demonstrate patience. The patience displayed by friends can help solidify a relationship or allow it to unravel.

In life, there are actions and reactions; we face those done by others to us, and we respond in kind. Let's face it — we can never be in control of those things said or done by others to us. If it's a harsh word or insult, or a G-d-given situation of life which may be particularly difficult, we can't control the set of circumstances that we're given. However, the way *we* respond, what *we* say, and *our* attitude is totally within our control.

Very often, the situation which we are faced with can fill us with a sense of frustration or anger. Sitting in traffic for an hour can be taxing on our patience, and being insulted makes us angry. Confronting the circumstances calmly means that we have thought out the consequences of our actions. We will act with our mind, not just our emotion, Not lashing out at someone who may have hurt us doesn't show a weakness of character; to the contrary, it shows tremendous inner strength. With a patient and well thought-out response, we can turn a potentially difficult situation into an opportunity for personal growth.

Calmly confronting every situation does not mean being complacent with one's station in life. One must constantly be vigilant to make sure that he or she is not coasting, leading life in "spiritual cruise-control". Knowing that we have spiritual progress to strive for, will ensure that we are always interested in bettering ourselves. Accepting mediocrity in matters of the soul and character will ultimately not lead to our emotional growth.

סדר
Order

To carry out one's responsibilities in a neat and orderly fashion.

The Alter (Elder) of Novardhok (1848-1919), Rav Yosef Yozel Horowitz, was one of the giants of the *Mussar* movement, which espoused character development and self-examination. Wishing to visit his son who was learning in a yeshiva some distance from Novardhok, he took the lengthy trip to inquire about his child's spiritual development.

"Please show me my son's room," the Alter said to the yeshiva student who was his escort. The student was puzzled that the Alter didn't ask to be taken to the study hall to ascertain his son's progress or perhaps speak to his teachers. The Alter soon explained his actions. "I came to my son's room and found his clothing and belongings in a neat and orderly fashion. Once I saw that his mundane affairs were being maintained properly, I had no doubt that his spiritual affairs were most certainly in order!" The trip to the study hall became unnecessary.

Order also involves putting a priority on those actions which are important, and less emphasis on those which are not. On Passover, we celebrate the *Seder*. The word connotes not only the order of the rituals to be performed on the night of Passover, but the commentators expand its definition. The order of the whole year is encompassed in the two nights of Passover. Concepts of freedom and servitude come clearly into focus. Are we truly free to pursue meaningful goals in life? Do we emphasize the many constructive opportunities that life has to offer, or do we find ourselves enslaved by the day-to-day activities which move us away from our intended goal? The order that a person maintains in her everyday affairs will enable her to prioritize her life, and find meaning and substance in everything she does.

ענוה
Humility

To recognize one's shortcomings and disregard those of one's fellow man.

A great Chassidic rebbe said, "We are created with two eyes; one to see our own faults and the other to see our friend's positive qualities." The words of the verse וְאָהַבְתָּ לְרֵעֲךָ כָּמוֹךָ אֲנִי ה' —"You shall love your fellow as yourself" (*Leviticus* 19:18) allude to this concept. By what standard do we judge ourselves? If we always try to minimize our own faults, because of our self-love, we should at least look at our friend in the same gracious manner.

Moshe was called an עָנָו, exceedingly humble, more so than any person on the face of the earth (*Numbers* 12:3). How can this be the title for the only individual who ascended into the heavens, received the Torah and was always available to hear the word of G-d? Moshe recognized his own personal qualities, knowing that they were all gifts from the Al-mighty. It's *because* Moshe was so great and was so close to G-d that he was in fact so humble. When we are in the presence of greatness, we feel very small in comparison.

The smarter we are, the more talent we possess, the more success we achieve, the more we should truly feel humble. If we recognize that G-d is the Source of these many gifts, we begin to think: "Have I adequately thanked and appreciated all that I have received from Him?" If we are proud of what we have done with our talent or resources, we must recognize the reason for these blessings. Additionally, the better we become, the greater is our responsibility to do even more. G-dly gifts are a challenge as well as a responsibility. In our interpersonal relationships, the more positively we view our fellow man, the more favorably we will be looked upon by G-d.

Justice as the Sages interpret; to give of your own even when not required.

When we give צְדָקָה, charity, we are doing so much more than helping an individual in need. The root of the word is צֶדֶק, righteousness. The Torah mandated giving to the destitute because it is a just and proper way of upholding the world and following G-d's precepts. The *Midrash* (*Vayikra Rabbah* 34:10) says: "More than the host benefits the poor man, the poor man benefits the host." G-d will ultimately provide for the needs of the poor in some way. G-d, Who bestows life, will also provide for man's sustenance in an abundant or a meager fashion. The poor man, however, serves an important function for his bene-factor. By being a beneficiary of his kindness, he has enabled the charity- giver to find an outlet for his kindness, and thereby carry out the precepts of justice. The world is kept in balance when the givers give and the poor receive.

In Judaism, there is דִּין, justice, and לִפְנִים מִשּׁוּרַת הַדִּין, beyond that which the law requires. "Jerusalem was destroyed only becuase it judged according to the law, and not beyond the letter of the law" (Talmud *Bava Metzia* 40b). If we act with strict justice, unbending in our ways, we call Divine justice down upon our actions. If we do more than we are required, G-d, too, will judge us with an extra measure of compassion.

Sometimes people find it easy to give money to charity. A worthy cause will attract the support of many, and often people fulfill their charitable obligation with their checks. A discerning giver will look for ways to uphold the righteousness of the world with more than a monetary gift. Giving of one's time, giving by caring and feeling, can often do more to assist the poor person that the actual donation. A sense of communal obligation to emulate G-d's beneficence will assist the destitute, and create a better, more just world.

קמוץ
Thrift

Not to spend even a penny in a foolhardy manner.

Thrift, as outlined by Reb Yisrael Salanter, should not be confused with miserliness, which is a negative character trait. When Yaakov crossed over the ford of Yabok (*Genesis* 32:23), he remained alone. He had forgotten some small vessels on the other side and went back to retrieve them. Did Yaakov, who had amassed a tremendous amount of cattle and sheep in his years working for Lavan, need to be concerned over the value of a few small jugs? The Talmud (*Chullin* 91a) teaches us that the righteous hold their money dear to them because each penny is earned honestly.

Every penny that is earned by a person who is exacting in the laws of the Torah is a message of faith in G-d. The paltry sum that a righteous individual earned is no less Divinely ordained than a windfall profit in business. Each has G-d's unique imprint; the sums, small or large, were gifted by G-d to be specifically for this *tzaddik*, righteous person. A penny is as much a connection to the Al-mighty as 100 talents of gold.

The Talmud (*Bava Batra* 11a) relates that King Munbaz opened his granaries to his subjects during a year of famine. He was chastised for his waste by his brothers and members of his father's household. Munbaz's answers tells us about the importance of investing one's money. "My ancestors saved below and I am storing riches above, for eternity; my ancestors hid their treasures in a place accessible to man; I am placing them in a place where no human can take them. My brothers have amassed wealth in monetary terms; I have saved lives. My brothers have saved for others, while I have invested for myself. My brothers have invested in this world; I have invested for the World to Come.

If one spends even a small amount foolishly, he has lost an opportunity to connect himself to his Creator.

שתיקה
Silence

To consider the ramifications of one's words before speaking.

מִלָּה בְּסֶלַע שְׁתִיקָה בִּתְרֵין (מגילה יח.)

"One word is worth one *sela*, silence is worth two"
(Talmud, *Megillah* 18a).

What type of speech is the Talmud referring to? Certainly the reference must be to permissible speech, because forbidden speech has no positive value, and is most detrimental! (*Pele Yoetz*). Even the simplest conversation can be fraught with danger, possibly causing harm to your neighbor with an offhand remark or disparaging joke at his expense.

Man's speech is likened to an arrow: חֵץ שָׁחוּט לְשׁוֹנָם. *their tongues are like a drawn arrow (Jeremiah 9:7)*. In combat, when a warrior wields a sword, he has full control over the weapon. Once an archer releases his arrow, he has no control over the great damage it can cause at a distance. So, too, is our speech. We may, heaven forbid, utter disparaging words against someone in a far-off place, and the damage is far reaching. Once harmful words have been spoken, they can not be recalled.

In *Pirkei Avos*, Judaism's most complete volume of ethical teachings, Shimon says: "All my days I grew up among the Sages, and I have not found anything better for the person than silence" (*Pirkei Avot* 1:17). *Maharal* explains that thought is in the exalted realm of the mind, while speech involves the body. Matters of the soul should be given free reign, while silence is the key in matters of the body. *Rashi* comments, based on the phrase in Proverbs, "Even a foolish person who is silent can be thought of as wise." A wise person who constantly speaks will sometimes err in his speech. By understanding how important one's words are, an individual will often opt to remain silent, and weigh each word before speaking.

Allusions of Twelve

The number twelve is particularly significant to the Bat Mitzvah, as that is the age when she becomes a full fledged member of the Jewish people. In Judaism, there are many meaningful numbers, and the number twelve is no exception. There are seven days of the week and seven weeks in the *sefirah* period, the counting of the weeks from Passover till Shavuot. There are seven years in the *shemittah* cycle, when the Jews in Israel are commanded to leave the land fallow. There are four Matriarchs, four cups of wine, four sons and four questions on Passover.

What is significant about twelve, particularly in relation to Bat Mitzvah being the beginning of a young woman's role as a *halachic* adult? We also know the song that is sung at the end of the Passover Seder (if we're still awake!). "Who knows one? "I know One! One is our G-d, in the heaven and the earth." And the song continues to list the importance of all the numbers up until thirteen. "Who knows twelve?" "I know twelve! Twelve are the tribes (of Israel). If this song has attained a prominent place in the *Seder*, it must be important. Each of the numbers listed are those that helped create the foundation of the Jewish people.

What makes twelve a primary, fundamental number to be included with all the others, most of which are single digits? It would seem to be simply a combination of single numbers, of which there are no limit. Why was twelve chosen? Rav Shimshon Pincus, z"l (*Beraichot B'Cheshbon*), explains that twelve is a number which signifies building upon a foundation. It's a transitional number, connecting individual numbers to create a greater whole. $4 \times 3 = 12$ (eleven can't be made up of two digits multiplied with each other). There are three *avot*, Patriarchs, and four *imahot* Matriarchs. The foundation of the Jewish nation as a people were Abraham, Isaac and Jacob. Without the Matriarchs working with them, the potential of these three great men could never have been realized.

When we combine these powerful forces together, the building which is created is the Twelve Tribes. They didn't merely *add* to their greatness; they helped bring it to fruition by multiplying its effect. When the tribes traveled in the wilderness, all the tribes marched in formation. It wasn't single file or even double file, but there were four sides of three tribes each that completed the traveling formation.

The Twelve Tribes did not have the stature of the forefathers, but were the bridge, the transition in the formation of the Jewish nation. The structure of the Jewish people had now taken form, as the building to take shape. Each day is built from twelve hours, as that forms its structure. The year is a composite of the twelve months of the year, comprised of the four seasons of three months each. The twelve signs of the zodiac, called *mazalot*, represent the sum total of astrological formations.

Bat Mitzvah – Transitions and Building

Building upon Rav Pincus's foundation, the age of twelve is a logical, as well as biological, transition period for the Bat Mitzvah. The period of the young girl's formative years has ended and now she crosses the threshold into adulthood. Interestingly enough, the young *man* has certain *halachic* considerations when he reaches twelve years and a day. Although he is considered a minor in basically every sense of the word, he has adult status regarding vows that he made. The child of twelve is responsible for upholding any vows he made at that age, assuming he is mentally cognizant, being aware of their binding nature and to Whom they were directed. This quasi-child, quasi-adult-status, called מוּפְלָא הַסָּמוּךְ לְאִישׁ (Talmud, *Niddah* 45b), is the transition phase between a child and an adult.

The early years of the young girl's childhood are complete now that she is twelve years old. The first stage of the building, בִּנְיָן, of her life has passed, and she is now prepared to embark on her life as an adult. The source in the Torah that alludes to an advanced maturity, at twelve rather than thirteen, is from a verse in Genesis, (בראשית ב:כב) וַיִּבֶן ה' אֱלֹקִים | אֶת־הַצֵּלָע, "and G-d fashioned the rib which He took from Adam into a woman" (Genesis, 2:22).

According to the Talmud (*Niddah* 45a), וַיִּבֶן refers to the additional בִּינָה, measure of understanding, in which a woman is superior to a man. A young girl achieves this at twelve; her male counterpart arrives at it a year later.

The apparent, simple meaning of וַיִּבֶן is He fashioned, or built, the rib of Adam into a woman. With the בִּינָה – the understanding – the בִּנְיָן, the newly formed building is now complete. The new materials for a young woman's future development have been given to her, and she now has the rest of her lifetime to bring them to fruition.

The early years of the young girl's childhood are complete now that twelve years have passed. The first stage of the building of life is over, and she is now prepared to embark on her life as an adult.

Chesed:

Touching Eternity
With Our Actions

Chesed – חסד
Lovingkindness

Why Did G-d Create an Imperfect World? That's Where We Come In!

Ever since the moment G-d breathed the spirit of life into man, every person alive carries within himself or herself a part of G-d. The soul, this Divine piece of Hashem, separates man from the rest of creation. And the highest expression of the soul comes through acts of *chesed* (lovingkindness).

If you saw someone crying, you would feel a tug inside – you'd feel compelled to help in some way. That's your soul talking. When a person performs an act of *chesed*, he is not only being nice, he's fulfilling the purpose for which we were all created. The Torah commands us to emulate Hashem, Who provides food for millions of plant and animal species, and arranges the precise and perfect combination of elements to enable the world to breathe, thrive, reproduce, and renew. He designed systems of minute precision to keep the chemicals of the body and brain in sync, as well as systems far beyond our comprehension that keep the entire universe in balance.

G-d reveals His nature through His constant care of His creation. We emulate Him by caring for our fellow man. Hashem could have created a world of self-sufficient people where no one would depend on anyone for anything. Consequently, no one would ever need to give of himself. G-d had other plans. He created each human being with gaps and deficiencies so that we would connect with and complete each other through constant acts of generosity. By doing acts of *chesed*, we cultivate the G-dliness within, keeping the Soul alive and releasing its radiant light into the world.

The truth is – *chesed feels good*. Giving to others engenders happiness – from the deep satisfaction of the Soul doing exactly what it was meant to do. *Chesed* also serves as a powerful protective merit for the Jewish People. The Torah instructs that when strict justice rains down from Heaven, we can minimize its force by showing compassion to one another. Our compassion inspires G-d's compassion.

Hashem could have created a world of self-sufficient people where no one would depend on anyone for anything. Consequently, no one would ever need to give of himself. G-d had other plans.

THE WORLD IS BUILT ON KINDNESS PSALMS 89:3

עולם חסד יבנה

כוס ישועות אשא

Chesed –Touching Eternity

עוֹלָם חֶסֶד יִבָּנֶה (תהלים פט:ג) — The world is built on lovingkindness (Psalms 89:3). From the beginning of Creation, mankind has seen G-d's kindness. There was no "need," as it were, for G-d to create a world filled with plants, animals and humans; He was the Master of the World before any of these came into existence. G-d, Who is the Ultimate Good, bestows goodness upon the world by imbuing each creature with life, and sustaining it during its lifetime.

The verse in Psalms speaks of, עוֹלָם, *a* world, rather than הָעוֹלָם, *the* world. The world is the magnificent combination of life, light, sound and color that we are privileged to be part of each and every day. The artistry that the Master Artist perfected is ours to enjoy.

G-d created the world as we see it; He allows <u>us</u> to be involved through our actions to build a life and a world that is uniquely ours and, thereby become His partner in creation.

Building Worlds

How does a young woman or man build a world? Like any building made by humans, one needs an architect's rendering to delineate the structure planned. What should it look like? Are the materials I have chosen the right ones for the job? Who will assist me in following the project through to completion?

Family members gathered in the home of the sainted Rav Yechezkel Levenstein (1885-1974), the venerable mashgiach, spiritual advisor, of the famed Ponevez Yeshiva in Bnei Brak, Israel. In the early sixties, a package from their relatives in America was reason enough for excitement. The simple trappings of the home and humble surroundings bespoke a lifestyle with few of the "luxuries" of their family in the States. Any gift that could make things a bit easier was always greatly appreciated.

The wrapping was discarded, and from the cardboard box a new kitchen appliance was removed, to the delight of all assembled. The mixer, its parts and the accompanying instruction book were laid out on the table, and Rav Yecheskel exclaimed, "This is proof that the Torah was given by G-d in heaven!" Though his family recognized that their American relatives were certainly Divine messengers for sending the package, they awaited the profound lesson the mashgiach would share.

"This appliance came from nearly 6,000 miles away," said Rav Yechezkel, "traversing a great distance to reach us.

The world is the magnificent combination of life, light, sound and color that we are privileged to be part of each and every day. The artistry that the Master Artist perfected is ours to enjoy.

As wonderful as it may be, this appliance would be absolutely useless to us – unless it was accompanied by the instruction manual on how to use it. The little booklet enclosed enables us to fully appreciate our relatives' gift.

"Man's soul, his neshamah, travels a much greater distance, being sent by G-d from beneath the Heavenly Throne of Glory. G-d's gift of life is implanted in the body of every Jewish child born.

"That gift, too, is wasted unless we utilize life's 'instruction manual' sent to guide us through life – the Torah."

The Torah was given by G-d to the Jewish people as a guide to living in this world. Each story recounted about the lives of the great people who shaped the destiny of our nation is really a profound lesson about the qualities needed to shape our lives and help build worlds. The 613 *mitzvot*, commandments, including 248 positive commandments and 365 prohibitions are the building blocks used. Each architect brings his or her own individual abilities or talents into play, drawing upon the unique resources and talents with which he or she was endowed.

As we embark on our venture, we'll discuss our plans and strategies with those who have had experience in building to create a more perfect structure. Our parents, grandparents, teachers, communal leaders and often peers are the role models and instructors from whom we can learn important lessons. Which approaches have been successful? What are the pitfalls in pursuing one direction over another? And most importantly, how can I use my unique, G-d-given abilities to build a better world for myself and those whose lives I touch?

Living for Myself – Living for Others

There is a distinct difference between the animal kingdom and the world of human beings. A horse or cow gives birth to its offspring, and shortly after entering the world, the foal or calf can stand on its own. Though they may rely somewhat on their mothers for negotiating their new world and obtaining food, they are very much self-sufficient. They roam about freely, like any animal many years their senior. שׁוֹר בֶּן יוֹמוֹ מִקְרִי שׁוֹר, "a day-old cow is still called a cow" (Talmud, *Bava Kamma* 65b). In the animal kingdom, the distinction between adults and children is minimal, as both are essentially self-sufficient.

Look at a baby when it is born. As cute as that little boy or girl is, it is virtually helpless without the assistance of others. It can't eat, walk, talk, take care of basic needs or change itself

How does one change from being a "recipient," one whose needs are totally catered to, to being a "giver," a sensitive, compassionate, giving individual?

without the help of its loving parents. We shower it with love and attention and jump to help at its every cry. Parents who have gone through sleepless nights caring for a colicky baby, or who structure their own lives around the life of a two week old baby, are happy to join the ranks of proud parents (though they are tired). They give selflessly for years: feeding, clothing, caring, nurturing, comforting, teaching, loving, directing, protecting and more — and often they'll be content with just a smile in return.

Let's think about it. In every generation since the beginning of Creation, the scenario has repeated itself. Animals are born and are basically self-sufficient, and babies are born and are totally dependent! Parents continue to give of themselves to those they love. In Hebrew, the word for love is אֲהַבָה, *ahava*. Rav Eliyahu Dessler, in his classic work *Michtav MiEliyahu*, points out that the root letters of the word is הַב, the Aramaic word for "give." Parents give unconditionally to those they love, and the more they give, the stronger grows the bond between parent and child.

Every boy and girl is created as totally dependent individual. They are waited on for their every need. Initially, it is their parents who provide for them, and as they grow, their circle of providers expands to include family, friends, teachers and community.

And there is an inherent danger in this Divinely directed system. How does one change from being a "recipient," one whose needs are totally catered to, to being a "giver," a sensitive, compassionate, giving individual? Though we all know people who are inherently *giving* individuals, seemingly always there to help others, generally a great deal of work is needed to overcome the constant life as recipients in their childhood.

Myself and Others

אִם אֵין אֲנִי לִי מִי לִי וּכְשֶׁאֲנִי לְעַצְמִי מָה אֲנִי — "If I am not for myself, who will be for me; and if I am only for myself — what am I?" (*Pirkei Avot*/Ethics of the Fathers, Chapter 1:17). The great sage Hillel, author of this message on life and interpersonal relationships, seems to pose two diametrically opposite statements! The first statement seems to focus totally on *my* needs; if I don't look after myself, then who will? Though it may seem to be egotistical, it states a fairly obvious reality, that one must look out for his own well-being. The second half of Hillel's teaching seems to point beyond the "me" in life. If I only think of myself, says Hillel, then of what benefit am I?

Rav Shimon Shkop (1859-1943), great rabbi and teacher for nearly sixty years in the Yeshiva of Grodno, Poland, offers a fascinating insight into this apparent contradiction (introduction to *Shaarei Yosher*). Man can look at the need to do for "me" in an extremely limited sense. On the most basic level, one can take care of his personal, physical needs exclusively. "I" am taken care of when my physical needs are satisfied. A more refined individual recognizes that the "I" is more than a body, and the needs of my soul must be addressed as well. A more expansive definition of "I" includes my wife and family. It would be callous to advance one's physical, and even spiritual elevation at the expense of the well-being of one's family.

The exalted "I" of which the *mishnah* speaks is the most all-encompassing. There is no line of demarcation between my needs and those of the community of Jews. I see myself as one limb of an entire body. What affects my limb affects the whole of the body. Any one part of a machine affects its entire operation and is crucial to its proper functioning. My definition of "I" takes on a much greater significance. "If I am not for myself, then who will be?" If I look at life with a Torah-true perspective, then my personal needs and those around me do not conflict. My new definition of self encompasses myself, my family and the entire Jewish people.

If I do for others in the community, in effect, I am doing for myself. I give a poor person a contribution not merely to assuage my personal feelings of guilt, but to address my collective responsibility for the needs of the greater Jewish people. My needs and "their" needs become one and the same, working together towards a higher goal.

Women and the Role of Chesed

Men and women are obligated to perform acts of *chesed*. The Torah begins with G-d's act of *chesed* to Adam by clothing him with garments, and ends with *chesed* as G-d involves Himself, as it were, in the burial of Moses. *Chofetz Chaim* (1838-1933), in his classic work, *Ahavas Chesed*, discusses three aspects of doing *chesed*. The first is an outgrowth of our fear of Hashem. "And now, Israel, what does G-d ask of you, but to fear Hashem ... to go in all His ways and to love Hashem" (*Devarim* 12:12). Our awe of Hashem dictates that we follow His ways; just as He is compassionate, so, too, we should be. Our love of Hashem takes us to a higher level. We love Hashem — therefore we wish to emulate Him. The highest level is דְּבֵיקוּת בַּהּ, cleaving to Hashem. Our every action reflects a higher sense of purpose and a greater connection to G-d.

All of us, men and women, can hope to emulate the qualities of Hashem, ultimately attuning our actions to G-d's will. Men are obligated in Torah study for its own sake while women are not, although they must be well versed in the *mitzvot* that apply to them. דְּבֵיקוּת, cleaving to G-d presumes a greater degree of sensitivity — understanding the needs of others.

"A woman has a more discerning eye regarding guests than does a man" (Talmud, *Berachot* 10b). Since she is in the home more than the man of the house, she is more attuned to the needs of the poor as well. While a man would give a coin to a poor person (who would have to trouble himself to go buy food), a woman could immediately satisfy his needs by giving him food (Talmud, *Ta'anit* 23b). If women possess this greater understanding, then they can excel in their ability to channel this innate quality for the benefit of others.

אהבת חסד - The Love of Chesed

The Chofetz Chaim in his classic work *Ahavas Chesed* (Volume II, chapter 1) explains the verse in *Michah* 6:8. G-d has told us what is good and what He requests of you; to do justice and to love lovingkindness, *chesed*. There is an intrinsic difference between *doing chesed* and *loving chesed*. If a poor person approaches you one time, and then another, it becomes uncomfortable to avoid him. You toss him a coin to allay your discomfort, and you are "compelled" to give him charity. One who loves *chesed* does so in an open, giving way. Though one must provide for the material needs of his son, he appreciates the opportunity to provide for him, and is happy to bestow as much goodness as possible upon him. Loving *chesed* means looking for opportunities to perform it, running after it, rather than waiting until a need arises. We act with our fellow man in a loving, caring and compassionate way, and Hashem in kind will be favorably inclined to judge us with *chesed*.

When one has a love for a person or thing, he will not be satisfied with a limited relationship. If a child is away at school, every opportunity to call, write or see that child is another chance to display the parents' love. So too with *chesed*. One should never feel that "I've done all my *chesed* for the week or month"; one should seek daily opportunities for *chesed*. A day that goes by without engaging in *chesed* is a day that has not been utilized to its full extent (*Chofetz Chaim, Ahavas Chesed*, chapter 12).

Loving chesed means looking for opportunities to perform it, running after it, rather than waiting until a need arises.

Making Chesed a Habit

The Rabbis in *Pirkei Avos*/Ethics of the Fathers (chapter 3:19) gave us an insight into how the world runs. הַכֹּל לְפִי רוֹב הַמַּעֲשֶׂה, everything depends on the abundance of actions. While some commentators say that the *mishnah* is encouraging us to perform many actions to reap ultimate reward, Rambam offers a fascinating insight. Maimonides states: "A person who gives one person a $1,000 donation is inferior to one who gives one thousand people one dollar each." While certainly a $1,000 donation is more beneficial for the recipient than a much smaller amount, the effect of *giving* one thousand separate acts of charity has a tremendous impact on the giver! To give a donation is a singular act; to keep giving makes the action part of the person's character make-up.

The *mishnah* further tells us in *Pirkei Avot* (chapter 4:2) that one *mitzvah* leads to another. While the performance of one act of kindness does not necessarily ensure that he or she will follow with another, a climate of *mitzvah* performance is created (*Rav Chaim of Volozhin*).

Imagine the following scene. You and your parents are driving in a car in bumper-to-bumper traffic. The heated tempers of motorists surpasses the heat of the hot summer day. Suddenly, a driver is kind enough to let you into his lane, ahead of his car, as you approach a tunnel. You are touched by his kindness. As another car edges *his* way towards the tunnel, you graciously allow *him* to go ahead of you, remembering your fellow motorist's kindness. The scene (hopefully) repeats itself, as one person's kindness sets off a chain reaction, as one *mitzvah* leads to another.

The story is told of an energetic, idealistic young man named Yisrael Meir. In his youth, he pledged, "I am going to change the world!" He grew a little older and a little wiser, and he limited the scope of his efforts, seeing that his initial task was too daunting. "I'm going to change my country!" he thought. That task also began to seem too challenging. "I'll at least change my city," he enthusiastically proclaimed. Again, the obstacles were overwhelming. "Certainly I can change my immediate neighborhood," thought Yisrael Meir. He was frustrated by his failure, time and again. "Perhaps ... perhaps I can impact my family." There, too, he met resistance.

"When I realized that this approach didn't work, I decided to change my approach," he said. "I'm going to work to change *myself*. Once I saw that my efforts there were successful, I was able to positively change my family, my neighborhood, my city, my country — and the world!" Indeed, Yisrael Meir Kagan,

known as the great Chofetz Chaim, changed himself – and changed the world.

It's true. We can affect all of our surroundings, but we have to start with ourselves. We become the primary form of our activity in life, and the ripple effect of our actions goes far beyond ourselves.

Defining Chesed

Chesed, acts of lovingkindness, is responding to the needs of the recipient, more so than addressing what *I* can do for them. Imagine the following scenario: Mrs. S. is a masterful baker. Her cakes are delicious, and each is a beautiful, artistic creation. Every festive occasion is the community is enhanced by her culinary talents. Mrs. W. has to spend some time in the hospital, and her friend decides that one of Mrs. S's cakes would be the *perfect* homecoming gift. Expense is not considered, and a beautifully gift-wrapped cake, designed specifically for the occasion, awaits Mrs. W. as she returns from the hospital.

This seems like the perfect, thoughtful *chesed*. The only problem is that Mrs. W. is a diabetic. It was a touching gesture of love, but it truly wasn't what Mrs. W. needed.

Rav Moshe Leib of Sassov said he learned the true meaning of *chesed* from a conversation he overheard from two peasants.

A highly intoxicated Moishele was crying to his friend, Yankele. "Yankele," slurred Moishele. "Do you love me??"

Yankele was puzzled.

"Love you? Of course I love you!"

Moishele continued his barrage.

"Yankele, do you really *really*, love me??"

Frustrated, Yankele exclaimed, "Yes, yes, I really *really* love you! Why can't you believe me?"

Moishele paused, and asked his dear friend. "Yankele, so tell me, what do I need? Tell me, please, what do I need?"

Now Yankele was truly perplexed.

"What do you need? What do you need? Well ... how should *I* know what *you* need?"

"Aha!" exclaimed Moishele. "If you *really* loved me, you would know what *I* need!"

Rav Moshe Leib witnessed, from a most unlikely source, the defining aspect of what love and *chesed* is all about. We love our family, our friends, indeed any person, and try to address *their* needs with our actions.

We love our family, our friends, indeed any person, and try to address their needs with our actions.

Creative Chesed

The hallmarks of a Jew are that we are רַחְמָנִים בַּיְישָׁנִים וְגוֹמְלֵי חֲסָדִים (יבמות עט.), compassionate, bashful and perform acts of *chesed*. Many of the most prominent community-based *chesed* organizations in the Jewish community are a result of caring individuals who sensed a need — and acted upon it. While not every Jewish community is as heavily concentrated as New York, some of the many activities that take place give one a glimpse into the kindness that one Jew extends for another, regardless of where along the spectrum of observance that person may be.

When it was seen that the emergency response team of the city couldn't respond quickly enough, *Hatzolah*, a community-based emergency medical organization, was created. Medics, paramedics and highly trained volunteers selflessly save lives, at any time of the day or night. Not everyone can maintain a decent standard of living and afford the necessities of delicious Shabbat food, particularly because of the tight economic climate or one's fixed income. *Tomchei Shabbos* delivers large packages of Shabbat staples every Thursday night, and before every holiday. The package is dropped at the door, and the volunteer driver leaves hurriedly and anonymously, to protect the dignity of the needy recipient. Visiting and staying near one's loved ones when they are in the hospital can be difficult, particularly for Shabbat or Yom Tov. *Rivkah Laufer Bikur Cholim* and other community organizations make apartments available, complete with Shabbat amenities, near many New York hospitals. These are but a few of the opportunities that the Jewish community, *your* community, has created. The needs are great, but so is the caring, and the lives of so many are positively affected.

The Gemach – Investments in Chesed

The Chofetz Chaim in *Ahavas Chesed*, discusses the advantages of creating a *gemilat chesed*, a revolving *chesed* endeavor. By working with a capital investment and continuously lending and repaying, the efforts are maximized and the *chesed* increased. Some *gemachs* work with loans of money, interest-free (lending with interest is prohibited by Torah law). If the fund starts with $10,000 and makes loans of $500 each, 20 people can benefit. The loans are repaid after the designated time and another 20 people borrow. The scene keeps repeating itself, and the same principle creates multiple acts of *chesed*!

"But I don't have $10,000, even if I saved up all my allowance and baby-sitting money!" you lament. Money isn't the only type of *gemach* available. In New York, *Hakhel*, a community-based group compiled a list of *gemach* programs that they knew of – and the list was over *200 individual programs*. Creative *chesed* means trying to share the items, resources or talents that we have available with those who can benefit from them.

Some of these free-loan or *mitzvah* programs included:

- car seats
- children's furniture
- Purim costumes
- children's books
- audio tapes
- medical equipment
- folding beds
- wedding gowns
- flatware for *simchot*

- linen *gemach*
- leftover food from *simchot*
- mourning chairs
- toys and games
- floral arrangements
- beeper *gemachs*
- computer *gemach*
- Sewing *gemach*

... and the list goes on.

We've all been blessed, each with our own unique abilities, talents and resources. Hopefully, we can channel them into creative *chesed* opportunities, for ourselves and for the Jewish nation.

Chesed, An Integral Part of our Educational Curriculum

Schools across the globe have instituted *chesed* programs as essential components of their school syllabus. The Chofetz Chaim Heritage Foundation, based in Monsey, New York, has a *B'Drachov* division which produced a comprehensive *chesed* Program Idea Book for educators. These includes dynamic lesson plans devised to instill in students a deep and active love for other Jews. The curriculum provides practical activities that incorporate acts of kindness throughout each day of a person's life and contains a yearly calendar helping the students focus on areas of character development each month. Now that's using one's time wisely!

The following examples, selected from a number of girls' schools, poignantly demonstrate some of the ways young women are making *chesed* an integral part of their lives. May they inspire all of us to make our own unique and vital impact.

We've all been blessed, each with our own unique abilities, talents and resources. Hopefully, we can channel them into creative chesed opportunities, for ourselves and for the Jewish nation.

Adopt a Bubby – *Bikur Cholim* organization provides the school with a list of elderly clients and homebound individuals who could use regular visits and help with errands. The girls bring their warm, friendly presence to these grateful "bubbies" and make sure to keep in touch with them throughout the year.

Feeding Program – A group of girls visit a geriatric center to feed the elderly and offer them smiling faces and caring hearts to lift their spirits.

Shabbat Nursing Home Visits – Every Shabbat afternoon, after helping to clear the Shabbat table, a group of girls walk together to a local nursing home to visit the ailing residents. The cheerful exchange of talk and laughter adds Shabbat joy to what would have been a lonely, isolated day.

Tutoring Program – Girls volunteer to tutor students (in a myriad of subjects) who can't afford to pay a professional teacher.

Outreach – Every Friday morning (*erev* Shabbat) a group of girls visit a local school to lead a lively discussion on the *parshat hashavua*, the Torah chapter of the week, with girls new to Torah Judaism. They also invite the students to their homes for Shabbat and for a festive Motzei Shabbat *Melave Malkah*, a celebrative gathering with family and friends – bidding Shabbat a loving goodbye until the following week.

Respite Program – Girls volunteer to relieve parents who must be with their children in the hospital. They offer to stay with the child so that the parent can take a much-needed break.

Special Bnot – Whether one on one, as a team, girls take developmentally disabled women (at group homes in the community) for an enjoyable walk on Shabbat and to a Bnot group, where they sing, tell stories, and delight in each other's company.

Mother's Helper – If a mother is not feeling well or needs to go to the hospital, girls volunteer to help with whatever needs to be done at home including, child care, errands, and household duties. Mothers of twins or triplets also receive a helping hand(s).

Tomchei Shabbos – The girls help pack scores of Shabbat and *Yom Tov* food packages to be delivered to needy families throughout their community.

Peer Tutoring – Girls volunteer their time to tutor fellow classmates who are having difficulty with school subjects – helping them to strengthen their academic skills and their confidence.

Special Sports Program – Throughout the school year, every other Sunday, girls join in sports activities with the girls of *Yachad,* an NCSY (National Congregation of Synagogue Youth) outreach program for the developmentally disabled.

Toys for Children of Israel – Girls collect toys and art supplies from people throughout their community to send to children in hospitals in Israel.

"Bridges" After-School Mentoring – An after-school program where girls become caring "big sisters" investing valuable time with younger immigrant children helping them feel part of the greater Jewish family, as they acclimate to life in America.

Art & Heart Get Together – The girls invited Senior Citizens from Jewish Association for Services for the Aged (JASA) to join them at school for a joint arts & crafts session, followed by a friendly luncheon – sharing invaluable time of camaraderie, creativity, and a lot of warm cheer!

The Power of Unified Tehillim – (Psalms) – Throughout the years of Jewish struggle, both personal and communal, King David's heartfelt outpouring to Hashem continues to serve as a mighty key to opening the gate of compassion Above. Each day, girls divide the chapters among themselves – completing the entire book. At the close of their recitation a list of seriously ill Jewish men and women are read.

Thank you to The Chofetz Chaim Heritage Foundation, NY, Machon Bais Yaakov of Brooklyn, NY, Manhattan Day School, NY, Joan Dachs Bais Yaakov of Chicago, and Yeshiva University High School for Girls (Central) of Queens, NY for sharing their impressive chesed programs.

Chesed, Chicken and Side Dishes

In the areas of the country with large concentrations of Jews, opportunities for *chesed* abound. The truth is, that *every* community can be involved in a meaningful way if it seizes the chance to do so. A Brooklyn-based rabbi was casually discussing a community-based project which began to address a growing need. Despite the perception that "Jews are comfortable," difficult economic times had fallen on many families. Making ends meet from week to week was a challenge, and providing for the extras that Shabbat required seemed almost out of the question.

In the Flatbush section of Brooklyn, concerned individuals wished to help their friends who were having difficulties, in a discreet way. An ad-hoc committee was formed, and the list of families who made "another chicken and kugel" for a family in need grew — as did those who needed it.

In a quiet way, the need was being addressed, but the ripple effect was quite amazing. Thursday nights in the Kaszirer home in Brooklyn were a beehive of activity. Cars pulled up delivering "*chesed* chicken," and the accompanying side dishes that made Shabbat beautiful and complete for those who benefited. The beauty of the *chesed* was that it wasn't limited to the mother of the home, but the *chesed* became a family affair. The mother would make the chicken, an older daughter was in charge of kugels, the father would drive it over to the drop-off location, and a younger son would bring it to the house.

In Judaism, one *mitzvah* leads to another (Pirkei Avos 4:2). The casual reference of the Brooklyn rabbi to a friend who lived in a community 1500 miles away, about the Brooklyn *chesed* teams found a receptive ear and a willing heart. There are no geographic boundaries for economic hardship. The friend who heard about it wondered about implementing a program in her suburban neighborhood of Chicago. People would donate towards one course or another, and the distribution of the complete Shabbat packages would be efficiently administered by an existing community organization. Much work needed to be done, planning had to be executed and the newfound project—begun by an enthusiastic mother *and* her soon-to-be Bat Mitzvah daughter — would soon be a reality.

Shabbat Sunshine was born.

A comment. An idea. A healthy dose of enthusiasm. *Mitzvah* upon *mitzvah*. Teaching generations about *chesed* by example. The *Chesed* chicken is ready, and the side dishes are too numerous to count.

A Year of Chesed

icture the following scenario. A friend of yours is home from school. Though some of her friends assume that "she'll probably be back tomorrow," you take the time to find out if she's feeling well. Your thoughtfulness is greatly appreciated, as is your visit, "just to say hello." In your own small way, you have helped in the healing process, adding *chesed* upon *chesed*. Your act of kindness on Monday may be differently crafted for another person's needs on Tuesday, and still another on Wednesday. There may be many more than one *chesed* you'll be involved with daily, but try to make sure that a day doesn't go by without *chesed*. Your day will be different, your week will be different – *you* will be different!

Multiply this by all the girls in the class that are working on *consciously* being involved in *chesed* and the results are unbelievable. Go out of your way to help a friend, bring a smile to a homebound elderly person, do a kindness to a little brother or sister (that's *chesed*, too!), call someone to show you care — and you're building a better world!

If we look carefully at the Torah, we find that *chesed* is an integral component of the way G-d runs the world. "The Torah begins with [G-d's actions of] lovingkindness, and ends with [G-d's actions of] lovingkindness" (Talmud, *Sotah* 14a). In the earlier portions of the Book of Genesis, it discusses how G-d clothed, as it were, the nakedness of Adam and Eve after they had sinned. The Torah closes with the recounting of how G-d, as it were, helped bury Moses. We are shown aspects of G-d's infinite *chesed* so we can pattern our lives on similar acts of kindness. "Just as He is merciful, so we should be merciful; just as He is gracious, so too, we should be gracious" (Talmud, *Shabbos* 133b).

To help initiate your year of *chesed*, fill in only one act of *chesed* that you perform each day. Trying to write in too many brings frustration and disappointment. From time to time, review the actions that you have done over time. Jot down the *chesed* in the designated area each day and look back at it from time to time. *Rosh Chodesh* is a good time to review your month of *chesed*, particularly because it's a special day for women (see *Rosh Chodesh* section). You'll be amazed at how much you can accomplish in one month, and will be anxious to start the new month with many new and creative *chesed* ideas.

> There may be many more than one chesed you'll be involved with daily, but try to make sure that a day doesn't go by without chesed. Your day will be different, your week will be different — you will be different!

A word about this project, and with life in general. Be realistic with your goals, and don't be disappointed if you don't accomplish everything you wanted to. The verse says:

נָפְלָה לֹא־תוֹסִיף קוּם בְּתוּלַת יִשְׂרָאֵל (עמוס ה:ב)

"She has fallen and will no longer rise, the maiden of Israel" (Amos 5:2).

The simple meaning of the verse is a sad commentary about the fate of the Ten Lost Tribes, implying that their exile is final and that they will never arise. Our Sages, however, see the verse as an uplifting testimony to the strength of the Jewish people. "נָפְלָה לֹא־תוֹסִיף, *She has fallen, and will do so no longer –* קוּם בְּתוּלַת יִשְׂרָאֵל – *Rise, maiden of Israel!"*

Every time we stumble, we have another chance to pick ourselves up again. Each challenge is an opportunity for renewed growth. There are no problems in life – only solutions! We begin every day with the phrase as part of the morning services...

מוֹדֶה אֲנִי לְפָנֶיךָ מֶלֶךְ חַי וְקַיָם שֶׁהֶחֱזַרְתָּ בִּי נִשְׁמָתִי בְּחֶמְלָה רַבָּה אֱמוּנָתֶךָ.

I gratefully thank You, living, eternal King, for You have returned my soul within me, compassionately – abundant is Your faithfulness.

The commentaries question the meaning of the last phrase, רַבָּה אֱמוּנָתֶךָ, abundant is Your faithfulness. Shouldn't the phrase read רַבָּה אֱמוּנָתֵנוּ, how great is *our* faith in *You*? In truth, the Rabbis say that each day is another statement of G-d's faith in each human being. We wake up each day, knowing that maybe yesterday wasn't as perfect as it could have been. Maybe I could have been nicer to my friend, more respectful to my parents, prayed to G-d with more concentration. And yet... G-d gives us another day, another chance to do it better. *Your* faith in *us* is great — despite our failings, You allow us to wake up each morning and try once more.

Each day is a new start, another opportunity to achieve. Keep this daily record, and you'll see that your Year of *Chesed* will build worlds — eternally.

The concept of doing a chesed a day is discussed in the Chofetz Chaim's classic work Ahavas Chesed. The Chofetz Chaim Heritage Foundation, in conjunction with Mesorah Publications has published a magnificent translation of the work also featuring a chesed planning calendar. Rabbi Paysach J. Krohn, noted speaker and author, has suggested recording each day's chesed as well. You may copy our Year of Chesed Planner to help you and your friends build a better world.

January

	Sunday	Monday	Tuesday	Wednesday	Thursday	Friday	Shabbat
Week 1							
Week 2							
Week 3							
Week 4							
Week 5							

February

	Sunday	Monday	Tuesday	Wednesday	Thursday	Friday	Shabbat
Week 1							
Week 2							
Week 3							
Week 4							
Week 5							

March

	Sunday	Monday	Tuesday	Wednesday	Thursday	Friday	Shabbat
Week 1							
Week 2							
Week 3							
Week 4							
Week 5							

April

	Sunday	Monday	Tuesday	Wednesday	Thursday	Friday	Shabbat
Week 1							
Week 2							
Week 3							
Week 4							
Week 5							

May

	Sunday	Monday	Tuesday	Wednesday	Thursday	Friday	Shabbat
Week 1							
Week 2							
Week 3							
Week 4							
Week 5							

June

	Sunday	Monday	Tuesday	Wednesday	Thursday	Friday	Shabbat
Week 1							
Week 2							
Week 3							
Week 4							
Week 5							

Bat Mitzvah Treasury / Mesorah Publications

July

	Sunday	Monday	Tuesday	Wednesday	Thursday	Friday	Shabbat
Week 1							
Week 2							
Week 3							
Week 4							
Week 5							

August

	Sunday	Monday	Tuesday	Wednesday	Thursday	Friday	Shabbat
Week 1							
Week 2							
Week 3							
Week 4							
Week 5							

Bat Mitzvah Treasury / Mesorah Publications

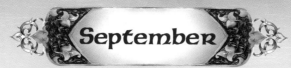

September

	Sunday	Monday	Tuesday	Wednesday	Thursday	Friday	Shabbat
Week 1							
Week 2							
Week 3							
Week 4							
Week 5							

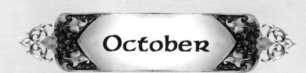

October

	Sunday	Monday	Tuesday	Wednesday	Thursday	Friday	Shabbat
Week 1							
Week 2							
Week 3							
Week 4							
Week 5							

November

	Sunday	Monday	Tuesday	Wednesday	Thursday	Friday	Shabbat
Week 1							
Week 2							
Week 3							
Week 4							
Week 5							

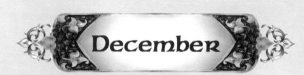

December

	Sunday	Monday	Tuesday	Wednesday	Thursday	Friday	Shabbat
Week 1							
Week 2							
Week 3							
Week 4							
Week 5							

Transitions:

Bat Mitzvah —
Coming of Age

Bat Mitzvah Observance and Celebration

A girl is obligated at twelve and must avoid transgressing Torah or rabbinic statutes at that age; a boy first comes of age at thirteen.

 girl becomes a *halachic* adult at twelve years and a day; a boy becomes a *halachic* adult at thirteen years old and a day. This holds true for Torah-based obligations, the performance of commandments, and transgressions of Torah or Rabbinic origin. A girl is obligated at twelve and must avoid transgressing Torah or rabbinic statutes at that age; a boy first comes of age at thirteen.

The Torah's statement (*Genesis* 2:22) about G-d fashioning the side, or rib, which He took from Adam, into a woman, is referred to as וַיִּבֶן, literally, He built. The Torah's use of וַיִּבֶן also relates to the word בִּינָה, understanding. Rav Chisda says that this teaches us that G-d gave an extra measure of understanding to woman, more than to man (Talmud, *Niddah* 45b).

As mentioned previously, the Talmud states that women were granted an extra measure of בִּינָה, understanding, generally interpreted by our Sages as מֵבִין דָּבָר מִתּוֹךְ דָּבָר, understanding one thing from another. This means an intuitive understanding rather than actually amassed text book knowledge. In truth, the physical maturity that considers her a *halachic* adult at twelve years old goes hand in hand with her intuitive maturity. Just as she develops physically more quickly than a male, so in the areas of spirit, her intuition and understanding, she is superior to him as well (*Torah Temimah*, Genesis 2:22).

The commemorative certificate on the facing page point to the significant aspects in the life of a young woman as she becomes Bat Mitzvah. The mitzvot of candle lighting, challah, tzedakah and the study of our traditional texts are all crucial to her development, for Torah and mitzvah observance are the hallmarks of a Jew. The day on which she becomes Bat Mitzvah is the culmination of twelve years of preparation and development. The certificate is crowned with the traditional blessing to daughters: may G-d make you like Sarah, Rebecca, Rachel and Leah.

ישימך אלקים
כשרה רבקה
רחל ולאה

את מצוה

ביום _____ On the _____

לחדש _____ Day of _____

שנת _____ In the Year _____

_____ _____

בת Daughter of

_____ _____

למשפחת Family Name

הגיעה לגיל המצות Became a
כבת מצוה Bat Mitzvah

_____ מקום Place _____

_____ עיר City _____

_____ רב/מורה Rabbi/Teacher _____

Bat Mitzvah Insights
Coming of Age

Since the festive *kiddush* celebration which marked her birth, the Bat Mitzvah is the first major milestone in the life of this Jewish young lady. Assuming responsibility to perform the *mitzvot* as an adult enables the Bat Mitzvah celebrant to overcome life's obstacles, and the G-d given ability to accomplish great things. This in itself is cause for celebration. Parents rejoice and call their friends and relatives to rejoice with them when a child is born. The rebirth which takes place when the young lady attains religious majority is indeed a cause for celebration.

What is the nature of the celebration, and what are we actually celebrating? We celebrate the conclusion of this stage of *chinuch*, instructional period of youth, confident that this young lady has learned sufficiently to manifest profound spiritual growth. The Bat Mitzvah should be so much more than a twelfth birthday party; it is a time to reflect on the years gone by, to take stock of what has been accomplished, and hopefully, assess aspirations for the future.

Friends and family shower gifts upon the celebrant, and sometimes, unfortunately, the acquisition of gifts and the festivities of the day become the focal point of the celebration. The greatest gift is the profound significance of the day. The young lady started the day as a little girl, and suddenly she is a young woman, a responsible member of our beloved people. The are no visible outward physical changes on the day of her Bat Mitzvah. Neither has she grown, increased her I.Q. or visibly become a different person. From the time that a young lady turns twelve years old (and a young man turns thirteen), they have attained majority status in every sense of the word. Based on the Oral Law given to Moses on Mount Sinai, these twelve- and thirteen-year-olds, respectively, accept the privileges — and responsibilities — of being a *halachic* adult.

Actions that could once be dismissed as "mere childish behavior" are looked at from a different vantage point. While Judaism recognizes that the social maturity of a twelve-year-old can't compare with a young lady many years her senior, the Bat Mitzvah is a time to examine and evaluate one's actions, direc-

> The greatest gift is the profound significance of the day. The young lady started the day as a little girl, and suddenly she is a young woman, a responsible member of our beloved people.

tions and values. The beautiful foundations that her parents, as architects, have laid for her, must be carefully built upon. Our young Bat Mitzvah celebrant is the primary builder of the life that she helps create for herself. Of course, parents, teachers and friends are always ready and willing to assist in the process, but the primary challenge is hers.

G-d has given each young woman the raw materials; her parents provide the framework in which she can create, and the young woman must exercise her craft to perfection. At times, the responsibility seems overwhelming. "How can *my* actions affect the world around me?"

A thought from the Talmud helps bring the concept into focus.

רְאֵה אָנֹכִי נֹתֵן לִפְנֵיכֶם הַיּוֹם בְּרָכָה וּקְלָלָה (דברים יא:כו). "See I have given you today a blessing and a curse" (*Devarim* 11:21). Many commentators note the change of tense from רְאֵה, see, in the singular, to לִפְנֵיכֶם, before you, in the plural. *Kli Yakar* points out that the Talmud (*Kiddushin* 40b) says that one should see the world as if it is evenly balanced, half on the side of merit and half on the side of guilt. If one does a *mitzvah*, he tilts the world's balance favorably. One transgression has a negative impact on the world. One person, one action — and the entire world is affected.

This is the message of the above verse. "You, as an individual, should see that your vision of a blessing and a curse is far-reaching and will affect the community as a whole. Imagine the frustration of drivers stuck in a hour-long traffic jam. Car after car is lined up waiting for the mess to clear, but to no avail. They inch forward at a snail's pace, only to discover the cause of the problem. *A single car* sits overheated in the middle of the road — and literally *hundreds* of cars sit impatiently because of it. One person, one car, one action — yet the effects ripple outward to impact on so many.

Your singular action makes you a better person, your community a more enjoyable place to live, and the world much better. As a minor, one's actions are personally important, yet as a Bat Mitzvah each action is weighed on a more exalted scale.

Becoming Bat Mitzvah

t should be noted that the proper term is *becoming* a Bar Mitzvah or Bat Mitzvah, rather than *having* one. The former connotes a state of being, indicating that because one is of age, he or she now takes upon him or herself the obligation and responsibility to be part of our Jewish nation, a *halachic* adult. "Jason had a great Bar Mitzvah" or "Sandra had an awesome Bat Mitzvah" are statements that usually relate to the actual festive celebration.

While all over the world Bar/Bat Mitzvah is often marked with a celebration of one type or another, the scope of this volume does not allow us to deal with that aspect. We hope to examine those areas which touch upon the entry of a young lady into the ranks of the Jewish people.

Attaining religious majority and joining the ranks of one's elders is certainly a cause for celebration, and such celebration should reflect the significance of the day. An event so important in the life of a young woman will hopefully leave a lasting spiritual imprint long after the temporal trappings have faded.

What is the purpose of a Bat Mitzvah celebration? Rav Yechiel Yaakov Weinberg, author of *Seridei Aish*, discusses the celebration of Bat Mitzvah from a historic and philosophical perspective. In earlier generations, love of Torah and the fear of Heaven filled almost every Jewish home. Young women were infused with positive attitudes towards keeping the *mitzvot*, and the air of every Jewish town was replete with the sound and smells of Judaism.

The pervasive influences of today's secular society necessitate different strategies to help a Jewish young woman develop. The way to help infuse these girls with the sacred customs and practices of authentic Judaism is through Jewish education. Rav Weinberg, sensitive to the challenges of the secular society to a young girl's growth, sought to minimize these effects by celebrating the time when she became responsible for the *mitzvot*. It would be an opportunity for the Rabbi to exhort her to fulfill her obligations of *mitzvah*-observance, as pertain to the woman of the home. Additionally, it would be a chance when the Bat Mitzvah celebrant would learn about her role in creating the nurturing environment of a Torah-true home.

In earlier generations, love of Torah and the fear of Heaven filled almost every Jewish home. Young women were infused with positive attitudes towards keeping the mitzvot, and the air of every Jewish town was filled with the sights and sounds of Judaism.

Bar and Bat Mitzvah: Sons and Daughters

In *lashon hakodesh*, the Holy Language of Hebrew, each term that is used by our Sages is a specific, well-defined term. The use of one word or one phrase as opposed to another, is particularly significant. The commentators discuss the use of the terms Bar Mitzvah and Bat Mitzvah, literally, the son and daughter of a *mitzvah*. Regarding one who deviates from the path of *mitzvot*, the term *ba'al aveirah*, literally, the husband, or master of sin, is used. Why is the term son or daughter used regarding a *mitzvah*, while a husband/spouse or master/servant relationship is used regarding sin?

The answer points to a young man or woman's role as a new member of the Jewish people. The early years of *chinuch*, education, when a child learns about the *mitzvot*, begin his or her relationship with the Torah and its commandments. Though not yet obligated by Torah law to observe G-d's instructions for life, they must nonetheless start the process. By the time they are twelve and thirteen, respectively, the relationship established is eternal. Even if one strays from the path charted by his or her parents, the bond is never severed. A son will forever be a son, and one's daughter is always his daughter. The relationship one has to the *mitzvot* will remain eternally, even if its observance is sometimes compromised. The relationship established when he or she became a *halachic* adult will stay for the rest of their lives, no matter what transpires.

The affinity one has for sin is much more tenuous. The relationship between husband and wife, or master and servant, can, if necessary, be terminated. If one sins because of a lapse of observance, or because he or she gives in to temptation, that "relationship" need not remain. The transgression does not become part of his essence. A spiritual flaw can be rectified by repentance, and one's relationship with G-d reestablished. One connects eternally to a *mitzvah* but is never comfortable associating with a transgression. One incorporates each commandment into his or her being, while attempting to divorce himself from any impediment to a relationship with the Creator.

Being a "son or daughter" of the *mitzvot* has another connotation as well. The child of a prominent individual prides himself or herself on the fact that they stem from a refined or exalted lineage. Even after they are grown, they cherish the familial bond. A proud parent takes pride in his child's accomplishments and a child is equally proud of the stature of his parents.

In *lashon hakodesh*, an accomplished scholar is not called a *chacham*, a wise person, but a *talmid chacham*, a wise *student*. In Judaism, the more one learns, the more one realizes that there is so much more to learn. If one *has* a Bar or Bat Mitzvah, then the sense of pride and connection lasts as long as the affair does. Certainly it is a significant celebration, but it is a singular milestone event. Once one *becomes* a Bar or Bat Mitzvah, it is a state of being. We remain faithful *bnei* or *bnot mitzvah* when we demonstrate our pride in fulfilling a *mitzvah*. Like the *talmid chacham* who keeps learning, the Bar or Bat Mitzvah keeps performing *mitzvot*. The process begins at twelve or thirteen, and hopefully, will last for a lifetime. The more we prove ourselves as "children" of the *mitzvot*, the greater is the *nachat* to our Father in heaven.

≈ ≈ ≈

She will find peace in her surroundings and, most importantly, peace within herself. She will meet the challenges and opportunities that each day and week will bring, fortified with the blessings of heaven and earth.

The two blessings found on the art piece on the facing page offer the secret for success in life. Years of preparation and investing all of one's energies are important ingredients for accomplishment, but the blessings of the Al-mighty and parents are integral for the development of a true *bat Yisrael*.

May G-d make you like Sarah, Rebecca, Rachel and Leah. This profound blessing, which peers out from behind thc candles is a parent's prayer to G-d that He endow this daughter with the beautiful traits of her ancestors.

Even a father's blessings need heavenly affirmation, and we invoke the holy words used by the *kohanim* when they blessed Jews through the ages.

May Hashem bless you and safeguard you. May Hashem illuminate His countenance upon you, and be gracious onto you. May Hashem turn His countenance toward you and grant you peace.

In these words lie the blessings needed for life. If the watchful Eye of G-d is turned toward a new member of Israel, she will merit the grace and love of those around her. She will find peace in her surroundings and, most importantly, peace within herself. She will meet the challenges and opportunities that each day and week will bring, fortified with the blessings of heaven and earth.

ברכת מצוה

ישא יברכך ה' וישמרך
יאר ה' פניו אליך ויחנך
ישא ה' פניו אליך וישם לך שלום

Traditions:

Perpetuating
Our Heritage

In the Holy Temple, a part of our produce was removed and given to the priestly family, the kohanim. (Numbers 15:18) A portion of the challah was given to the kohein. He was dependent on the largesse of the Israelites, and they in turn, needed his offerings as an atonement for the sins of the Jewish nation.

The blessing is only recited if the requisite amount of flour is used, approximately five pounds. One is required to separate challah even if less flour is used, but without a blessing.

Separating Challah

Blessed are You, Hashem our God, King of the Universe,
who has sanctified us by His commandments and commanded us
to separate the challah from the dough.

Boruch atah Adōnoy, Elōhaynu melech ha-ōlom, asher kidshanu
b'mitzvōtav, v'tzivanu l'hafrish challah min ha'isah.

Since Judaism advocates experiencing Shabbos, the best way to appreciate the mitzvah of challah is by making (and eating) it.

Ingredients

5 pounds flour, 1 cup oil, 3 tbsp. salt, 4 eggs
4 ounces fresh yeast, 4 cups warm water, 1½ cups sugar

Directions

Put flour, salt and sugar in a bowl, form a well in the flour.

Dissolve yeast into 2 cups of the warm water with 1 tbsp. sugar.

Pour into the well — let sit for five minutes until yeast bubbles.

Add oil, eggs and the rest of the water.

Knead well until the dough becomes smooth and elastic.

It should spring back when pressed with the fingertips.

When dough rises, separate a piece the size of an olive, and thoroughly burn it.

When more than 5 lbs. of flour are used, recite the blessing above.

Form loaves. Brush lightly with egg beaten with 1 tsp. of sugar.

Bake at 350° for 45-50 minutes until golden brown.

הפרשת חלה

בָּרוּךְ
אַתָּה יְיָ אֱלֹהֵינוּ מֶלֶךְ
הָעוֹלָם אֲשֶׁר קִדְּשָׁנוּ
בְּמִצְוֹתָיו וְצִוָּנוּ
לְהַפְרִישׁ חַלָּה מִן הָעִסָּה:

יְהִי רָצוֹן
מִלְפָנֶיךָ יְיָ אֱלֹהֵינוּ וֵאלֹהֵי אֲבוֹתֵינוּ
שֶׁהַמִּצְוָה שֶׁל הַפְרָשַׁת חַלָּה תִּתְחַשֵּׁב כְּאִלּוּ
קִיַּמְתִּיהָ בְּכָל פְּרָטֶיהָ וְדִקְדּוּקֶיהָ, וְתֵחָשֵׁב הֲרָמַת
הַחַלָּה שֶׁאֲנִי מְרִימָה כְּמוֹ הַקָּרְבָּן שֶׁהֻקְרַב עַל
הַמִּזְבֵּחַ שֶׁנִּתְקַבֵּל בְּרָצוֹן. וּכְמוֹ שֶׁלְּפָנִים הָיְתָה
הַחַלָּה נְתוּנָה לַכֹּהֵן וְהָיְתָה זוֹ לְכַפָּרַת עֲוֹנוֹת
כָּךְ תִּהְיֶה לְכַפָּרָה לַעֲוֹנוֹתַי. וְאָז אֶהְיֶה כְּאִלּוּ
נוֹלַדְתִּי מֵחָדָשׁ נְקִיָּה מֵחֵטְא וְעָוֹן. וְאוּכַל לְקַיֵּים
מִצְוַת שַׁבַּת קֹדֶשׁ וְהַיָּמִים הַטּוֹבִים עִם בַּעֲלִי
(וִילָדֵינוּ) לִהְיוֹת נִזּוֹנִים מִקְּדוּשַׁת הַיָּמִים
הָאֵלּוּ וּמֵהַשְׁפָּעָתָהּ שֶׁל מִצְוַת חַלָּה
יִהְיוּ יְלָדַי נִזּוֹנִים תָּמִיד מִיָּדָיו שֶׁל הַקָּבָּ"ה בְּרֹב
רַחֲמָיו וַחֲסָדָיו, וּבְרֹב אַהֲבָה, וְשֶׁתִּתְקַבֵּל מִצְוַת חַלָּה
כְּאִלּוּ   נָתַתִּי מַעֲשֵׂר וּכְשֵׁם שֶׁהִנְנִי   מְקַיֶּמֶת
מִצְוַת חַלָּה בְּכָל לֵב, כָּךְ
יִתְעוֹרְרוּ רַחֲמָיו שֶׁל הַקָּבָּ"ה
לְשׁוֹמְרֵנִי מִצַּעַר וּמִמַּכְאוֹבִים
כָּל הַיָּמִים
אָמֵן:

Fortunate is the one who happily detects a delicious scent emanating from the kitchen on erev Shabbat. Women have long ago taken on the custom of baking challah on Friday in honor of Shabbat and to fulfill the Torah mitzvah of separating challah from the dough.

The Laws of Challah

Fortunate is the one who happily detects a delicious scent emanating from the kitchen on *erev* Shabbat. Women have long ago taken on the custom of baking *challah* on Friday in honor of Shabbat and to fulfill the Torah *mitzvah* of separating *challah* from the dough.

One should separate the challah as follows:

- Take off a piece of dough the size of an egg, then recite the blessing *Baruch ata ... lihafrish challah min ha'eesa* while standing. One should then burn the piece until it is no longer fit for consumption.

- One is obligated to separate *challah* from the dough if it consists of wheat, barley, spelt, oats, or rye and if there are more than 2 pounds and 10 oz. of flour, but no blessing is recited unless a minimum of approximately five pounds of flour was used.

- One removal of *challah* is sufficient for many different types of dough. If the dough is in separate utensils one should uncover them and bring the utensils together so that they touch one another.

- In the case where each dough is less than the required amount, one should combine all of the dough into one utensil or cover them together with one cloth.

- One does not recite the blessing on separating the *challah* unless the dough is of thick consistency and will be baked. If the dough is a thin batter or it will be cooked, one should separate the dough, but a blessing is not recited.

The Laws of Challah

❧ One separates *challah* with the appropriate blessing only if the dough is kneaded with water. If one uses fruit juice, she should separate the *challah* without the blessing.

❧ If one inadvertently did not separate the *challah* before the baking, it can be done afterwards. *Challah* cannot be separated on *Shabbat*. However, one can separate *challah* on *Yom Tov* (the holidays) if the bread will be baked on that day. One cannot separate *challah* from bread baked before *Yom Tov*.

❧ If the individual realizes on *Shabbat* or *Yom Tov* that *challah* was not separated, she should leave over a piece of bread the size of an egg and burn it after *Shabbat*. This allowance only applies in the Diaspora (those living outside of Israel). In Israel bread may not be eaten at all if *challah* was not removed before *Shabbat* or *Yom Tov*.

❧ The *challah* should be separated by the owner of the dough or someone delegated by her. A child under the age of Bar/Bat Mitzvah or a non-Jew may not separate the *challah*. If after being separated the dough became mixed with the remaining dough a *halachic* authority should be consulted.

In the Holy Temple, a part of our produce was removed and given to the priestly family, the kohanim. (Numbers 15:18) A portion of the challah was given to the kohein. He was dependent on the largesse of the Israelites, and they in turn, needed his offerings as an atonement for the sins of the Jewish nation.

Shabbat Candle Lighting

BLESSED are You, Hashem, our God, King of the universe, who has sanctified us with His commandments and commanded us to kindle the light of Shabbat.

Boruch atah Adōnoy Elōhaynu melech ha-ōlam, asher kidshanu b'mitzvōtav v'tzivanu l'hadlik nayr shel Shabbat.

MAY IT BE Your will, Hashem our God, and the God of our forefathers, that You grace me (and my husband, and sons and daughters, and my father and my mother) and all my relatives, and give to us and to all of Israel a good and long life; that You remember us favorably and with a blessing; that You recall us with salvation and mercy; and that You bless us with plentiful blessings, that You make our homes complete, and that You should make Your Divine Presence dwell among us. Grant us the merit to raise children and grandchildren who are wise and understanding, who love Hashem and fear Him. Men of truth, holy offspring, who cleave to Hashem and who enlighten the world with Torah and good deeds, and with all work in the service of the Creator. I plead with You, Hashem, hear my prayer at this time in the merit of Sarah, Rebecca, Rachel and Leah, our matriarchs. And illuminate our candles that they may never be extinguished for ever and ever. And let Your Countenance shine upon us that we may be saved. Amen.

Y'HI ROTZŌN l'fonecho, Adōnoy Elō hai v'Elōhay avōtai, she-t'chōnayn ōti (v'et ishi, v'et bonai, v'et bnōtai, v'et ovi, v'et imi) v'et kol k'rōvai; v'sitayn lonu u'lchol Yisroayl chayim tōvim va'aruchim, v'tizk'raynu b'zichrōn tōvoh u'vrochoh, v'tifk'daynu bifkudat y'shu'oh v'rachamim, u'tvor-chaynu b'rochot g'dōlōt, v'tashlim botaynu, v'tashkayn Sh'chi-notcha baynaynu. V'zakayni l'gadayl bonim uvnay vonim chachomim u'nevōnim, ōhavay Adonoy, yiray Elōhim, anshay emet, zera kōdesh ba'Adōnoy d'vaykim um'irim et ho-ōlam baTōrah uvma-asim tōvim u'vchol m'lechet avōdat habōray. Ana shma et t'chinoti bo'ayt hazōt bizchut Soroh, v'Rivkoh v'Rochel v'Layoh imō taynu, v'ho'ayr nayraynu shelō yichbeh l'ōlom vo-ed. V'ho-ayr ponecho v'nivoshay-oh. Omayn.

סדר הדלקת נרות שבת

בָּרוּךְ

אַתָּה יְיָ אֱלֹהֵינוּ מֶלֶךְ
הָעוֹלָם אֲשֶׁר קִדְּשָׁנוּ בְּמִצְוֹתָיו
וְצִוָּנוּ לְהַדְלִיק נֵר שֶׁל שַׁבָּת:

יְהִי רָצוֹן

לְפָנֶיךָ יְיָ אֱלֹהַי וֵאלֹהֵי אֲבוֹתַי, שֶׁתְּחוֹנֵן
אוֹתִי (וְאֶת אִישִׁי, וְאֶת בָּנַי, וְאֶת בְּנוֹתַי,
וְאֶת אָבִי, וְאֶת אִמִּי) וְאֶת כָּל קְרוֹבַי;
וְתִתֵּן לָנוּ וּלְכָל יִשְׂרָאֵל חַיִּים טוֹבִים
וַאֲרֻכִים, וְתִזְכְּרֵנוּ בְּזִכְרוֹן טוֹבָה וּבְרָכָה;
וְתִפְקְדֵנוּ בִּפְקֻדַּת יְשׁוּעָה וְרַחֲמִים;
וּתְבָרְכֵנוּ בְּרָכוֹת גְּדוֹלוֹת; וְתַשְׁלִים בָּתֵּינוּ;
וְתַשְׁכֵּן שְׁכִינָתְךָ בֵּינֵינוּ. וְזַכֵּנִי לְגַדֵּל בָּנִים
וּבְנֵי בָנִים חֲכָמִים וּנְבוֹנִים, אוֹהֲבֵי יְיָ, יִרְאֵי
אֱלֹהִים, אַנְשֵׁי אֱמֶת, זֶרַע קֹדֶשׁ, בַּיְיָ דְּבֵקִים,
וּמְאִירִים אֶת הָעוֹלָם בַּתּוֹרָה וּבְמַעֲשִׂים טוֹבִים,
וּבְכָל מְלֶאכֶת עֲבוֹדַת הַבּוֹרֵא. אָנָּא שְׁמַע אֶת
תְּחִנָּתִי בָּעֵת הַזֹּאת, בִּזְכוּת שָׂרָה וְרִבְקָה
וְרָחֵל וְלֵאָה אִמּוֹתֵינוּ, וְהָאֵר נֵרֵנוּ שֶׁלֹּא
יִכְבֶּה לְעוֹלָם וָעֶד, וְהָאֵר פָּנֶיךָ וְנִוָּשֵׁעָה, אָמֵן:

As Shabbat begins, the tears and heartfelt requests of each Jewish woman ascend heavenward with the light of the Shabbat candles

Laws of Candle Lighting

- The candles should be lit specifically for Shabbat. If they were lit for any other purpose they should be extinguished and lit again solely in honor of Shabbat.

- Candle lighting for the entire household is generally incumbent on the woman of the home, since she is usually the one most involved in running it. The husband should be involved by setting up and preparing the candles to be lit.

- If the woman of the home will be away on Shabbat, her husband should light. If he is also away, a daughter above the age of twelve should light. If not, a boy over thirteen should light.

- If one plans to sleep at home but eat outside the home, two options apply. Preferably, the candles should be lit at home before Shabbat begins. However, this is only an option if some benefit is derived from the candles after nightfall. This would mean either before leaving or upon returning home one should derive benefit from the light of the candles. If this is not an option, one should arrive at his hosts' home before Shabbat, and light there.

- When at a hotel for Shabbat, one should light either in the hotel room or on his private table. At the very least the candlelight should be in a place that will benefit those sitting there. If this is not an option, one should additionally turn on an electric light in the room with the intent to fulfill their obligation of lighting candles. Regarding the blessing a competent *halachic* authority should be consulted.

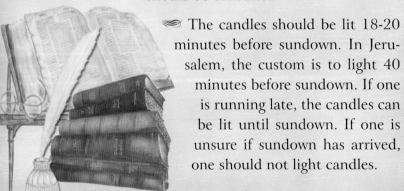

- The candles should be lit 18-20 minutes before sundown. In Jerusalem, the custom is to light 40 minutes before sundown. If one is running late, the candles can be lit until sundown. If one is unsure if sundown has arrived, one should not light candles.

The Laws of Challah

- The earliest time one can light candles is 1 ¼ hours before sundown (seasonal hours). If one lights before this time, he/she has not fulfilled the obligation and should light again with a new blessing. One should be especially aware during the summer months when accepting "early Shabbat" that they are lighting at the proper time.

- When lighting candles, one should hold the match or candle to the wick until the candle is fully lit.

- Blessings over *mitzvot* are generally recited immediately preceding the performance of the *mitzvah*. The accepted custom is to first light the candles, cover one's eyes (as not to benefit from the light until after recitation of the blessing), recite the blessing, and then uncover one's eyes and enjoy the light of the candles.

  In situations of need one may make a conditional acceptance of Shabbat enabling them to light candles without fully accepting Shabbat. A competent halachic authority should be consulted.

- The custom is to wave one's hands over the candles (towards oneself) before reciting the blessing after lighting, to usher in the Shabbat.

- The prevalent custom is to light two candles. Many add an additional candle for each child. However, if one is away from home, only two candles are lit.

- There is a time-honored custom that charity is given before candle lighting. Following candle lighting, it is an opportune moment to pray for the health and success of one's family.

- Customs vary as to when one begins the practice of lighting Shabbat candles. Generally it starts when a young woman is married. In some communities, it is begun when a girl becomes Bat Mitzvah; in others it is begun even earlier. Consult a competent *halachic* authority.

As Shabbat begins, the tears and heartfelt requests of each Jewish woman ascend heavenward with the light of the Shabbat candles

Tzniut: More than Meets the Eye

The physical self represents our external layer — our faces and our bodies — and can be called "what I have." Inside we carry the potential for talents and abilities, called "what I do." And at our very center, the very core, lives our soul — "who I am."

As human beings, we are complex creations composed of multiple layers. The physical self represents our external layer — our faces and our bodies — and can be called "what I have." Inside we carry the potential for talents and abilities, called "what I do." And at our very center, the very core, lives our soul — "who I am." If we are not careful, our external part could outshine and blind the world (and ourselves) to what makes us who we truly are.

Before the advent of clothing, Adam and Chava saw each other's outer and inner selves as one. They could easily perceive the radiance of their minds, hearts, and souls. After the severe and consequential mistake in the Garden of Eden, their vision was forever altered and obscured. Body and soul became two distinct entities. The physical and spiritual existed apart, disconnected from each other. The body's imposing presence blocked the holy light of the soul. From that moment on, it took a Herculean effort to identify a person beyond his or her outside. Yet all was not lost. According to our Torah, an active awareness of *tzniut* serves as the most effective way to reveal (and utilize) our true selves and unique strengths. *Tzniut*, commonly translated as modesty, gives us the ability to view ourselves far beyond and above how we appear on the surface.

As a person you are the most multifaceted creation of all. Upon meeting you for the first time people may immediately see "small build" or "curly hair." After spending a bit of time with you they may notice "creative" or "athletic." After really getting to know you, they may be able to see your compassionate heart, inquisitive mind, and noble spirit. The Jewish attitude of *tzniut* nurtures and preserves one's most valuable internal commodity, self-respect.

Guarding the Most Sacred

Often we fall into the trap of unconsciously defining ourselves solely by how we look. All too often the way we dress draws public attention to our outside, while completely disregarding the precious individual within. The current societal norm of dress (or lack thereof) projects a superficial message and does not reflect the true beauty and dignity of the individual inside. The more modest mode of attire advocated by Jewish sources sends the message: "I am much more than meets the eye. If you want to see the real me, look deeper, to my real content." This causes others to concentrate on one's authentic identity.

In order to convey this message, a woman must know how and when to reveal her physical self, her unique abilities, and everything else that makes her the person G-d created her to be. The challenge of *tzniut* is to project every aspect of oneself in such a way that it draws the focus, with the highest respect and appreciation, on whom one truly is.

A Goal for Both Men and Women

The Torah encourages both men and women to develop a heightened *tzniut*-consciousness. This mindset facilitates a deeper and more consistent spiritual view of the world. So, why is *tzniut* emphasized more for women than men? Women have an inherent propensity, an exceptional gift towards *tzniut* and can achieve great heights in this spiritual endeavor. A woman's sense of herself and the effect she has on those around her should come from the shining qualities within.

The Jewish laws of *tzniut* are not derived from a sense of shame of the body. Just the opposite. It is because the Torah regards the body as sacred that we treat it with the utmost dignity and respect. After all, the majority of the Torah's commandments are performed not by thought or feeling, but rather, through bodily actions. And the body serves as the home for the Jewish soul in this world.

Judaism connects hiddenness with G-dliness. What we deem as most precious, we keep concealed. In the holy Tabernacle in the desert, and later in the Temple, the holiest vessels were kept in the innermost chambers. In synagogues today, the Torah scrolls sit behind a curtain in a special, designated closet and are only taken out for specific use or repair.

The internal focus of *tzniut* cultivates a womanly strength and courage that can only be achieved when she looks to the inside — rather than the outside — for her self-definition. When a woman actively chooses to dress and behave in a dignified manner, she commands respect and frees herself to experience the person she truly is — most fully.

"If I am I, because I am I, and you are you, because you are you, than I am I and you are you. But if I am I because you are you and you are you because I am I, then I am not I and you are not you." *(Rabbi Menachem Mendel of Kotzk)*

Do we see ourselves through our own eyes, or as we wish to be seen by others? Do we need their approval to feel good about ourselves, or can we be confident in how we look and act without our friends' endorsement?

The Power of Tzniut

The most significant form of human power lives in the ability to effect change. A woman's internal strength of self-possession, insight and compassion holds the power to effectively touch, motivate, and heal another's heart, mind, and soul. Our Matriarchs exercised this inner force and affected the course of Jewish history. In secular society, success is defined in terms of external roles and concrete, quantitative achievements. As a woman focuses on excelling in the inner domain, she acknowledges the infinite value of growing as a person and helping others do the same. Jewish women throughout time used this invaluable inner resource to build those around them and bring the world closer to perfection.

When a Jewish woman presents herself with *tzniut*, she can more readily tap her very best qualities – with the grace and nobility befitting a daughter of the King.

The internal focus of tzniut cultivates a womanly strength and courage that can only be achieved when she looks to the inside — rather than the outside — for her self-definition.

The material for this essay has been adapted from the books Inside/Outside by Mrs. Gila Manelson and Our Bodies, Our Souls by Rebbetzin Tziporah Heller.

Time-Bound Mitzvot

There are two distinct categories of *mitzvot* in the Torah. The positive commandments, referred to as *mitzvot asei,* and negative commandments or prohibitions, referred to as *mitzvot lo taseh.* Examples of negative commandments include the mitzvah not to steal, not to swear falsely, and not to eat certain foods. The positive commandments are further subdivided into two distinct groups. *mitzvot asei shehazman gromo* those performed at specific times and *mitzvot asei shelo hazman gromo* those whose performance can de done any time. Examples of time-bound *mitzvot* include eating in the *succah* on *Succot,* and blowing the *shofar* on Rosh Hashanah. *Mitzvot* that are not time bound include honoring one's father and mother, and placing a *mezuzah* on one's doorpost. As a general rule, there are no differences between men and women concerning both the negative and positive commandments that are not time-bound.

The one group of *mitzvot* from which women, for the most part, are exempt include the time-bound positive commandments. Nevertheless women may and frequently do voluntarily observe many of the time-bound *mitzvot.* There are two basic reasons why women are exempt from time bound positive *mitzvot.* R' Samson Raphael Hirsch in his commentary on Torah explains as follows: "The Torah does not impose these *mitzvot* on women because the Torah does not consider them necessary demands on women. All of the time-bound *mitzvot* are meant to bring certain principles, ideas, and resolutions to our minds and to spur us and fortify us to keep them. G-d's Torah takes it for granted that women have greater fervor and more faithful enthusiasm to serve G-d. Accordingly, it does not find it necessary to give women these repeated reminders to remain true to their calling."

Abarbanel gives a second reason. The adherence to a rigid schedule that these *mitzvot* demand might conflict with a woman's primary responsibility as wife and mother, thereby threatening the harmonious relationship between husband and wife and the tranquility of the home that the Torah considers of paramount importance. For this reason the prevalence and degree of observance of these *mitzvot* is generally greater among single girls and married woman without children than those during the childrearing period.

שבת
Shabbat

Listed here are
the specific halachot,
laws that relate
to a woman's
performance of
time-bound mitzvot
on Shabbat and
the Festivals

Kiddush

"Remember the day of Shabbat to sanctify it." Although the positive Torah commandment to sanctify the Shabbat is a time-bound *mitzvah*, there is no distinction made between the obligation of men and women. This is based on the two verses that refer to Shabbat. One states "Remember the day of Shabbat," while the second states "Watch the Shabbat." The Talmud teaches us that "watching the Shabbat" refers to the prohibitions on Shabbat, while "remembering the Shabbat" refers to the positive commandments of Shabbat. The Talmud derives that all those included in the prohibitions of Shabbat are similarly included in the positive commandments of Shabbat. Regarding the observance of the prohibitions, there is no differentiation made between men and women, and therefore they are equally obligated in all of the positive commandments of Shabbat.

A woman may fulfill her obligation of *kiddush* either by reciting it herself or listening to *kiddush* from one who is similarly obligated. *Kiddush* is recited once prior to the Friday night meal and a second time prior to the meal on Shabbat day. After the onset of Shabbat one may not partake of food or drink prior to fulfilling the obligation of *kiddush*. The obligation of daytime *kiddush* begins after one prays in the morning. *Halacha* mandates that it is improper for one to eat before nourishing the soul with prayer. Before one prays on Shabbat morning, one should refrain from food or drink [with the exception of water, coffee, or tea]. After the completion of prayers, food or drink should be avoided until *kiddush* has been recited.

Shabbat Meals

Based on the fact that the Torah mentions the act of eating three separate times on Shabbat, the Talmud derives the obligation to eat three meals on Shabbat. The first meal is eaten at night, and two more are eaten during the day. Additionally, to commemorate the double portion of manna which fell on Friday for the Shabbat, the blessing of *hamotzi* should be recited on two whole breads. As with *kiddush*, a woman may either recite the *hamotzi* blessing or hear the blessing from one who is similarly obligated.

Havdalah

At the conclusion of Shabbat, one recites the *havdalah* prayer, describing the vast difference between the holy day of Shabbat and the other mundane days of the week. *Havdalah* is recited over wine, a fire from a special braided candle (with at least two wicks intertwined) and spices. One is not permitted to eat or drink before reciting or hearing the *havdalah* prayer

ימים טובים
Festivals

Rosh Hashanah

Women are not obligated to hear the blowing of the *shofar*, as it is a time-bound *mitzvah*. However, women throughout the generations have accepted upon themselves to fulfill this *mitzvah* whenever possible. One should wear less festive and expensive garments than on other festivals in recognition of the awesomenes of the Day of Judgment.

The blessing recited before candle lighting, *baruch atah.. lihadlik ner shel yom tov* is followed by the *shehechiyanu* blessing. There is a question whether one should recite the *shehechiyanu* blessing on the second night of the holiday. The most preferable option is to either wear a new garment or have a new fruit nearby which requires the *shehechiyanu* blessing – and to keep it in mind during the recitation.

Yom Kippur

It is a positive Torah commandment to eat on the day prior to Yom Kippur. Many *halachic* authorities are of the opinion that although a *mitzvah* bound by time, women are included. It serves as part of the requirement to fast on Yom Kippur, which obligates both men and women equally. A woman who is not fasting on Yom Kippur because of health considerations would not be included in the *mitzvah* of eating on the day preceding Yom Kippur.

Once a girl reaches the age of 9, she should refrain from eating somewhat into the day, adding additional hours with each year. Once she turns 11, assuming she is healthy, she should fast the entire day. Upon reaching the age of Bat Mitzvah, girls are required to fast the entire day. Children should be trained not to wear leather shoes on Yom Kippur. Women are required to recite the *vidui* [confession] on Yom Kippur.

Succot

Women are not obligated to eat in a *succah*, since it is a time-bound *mitzvah*. As with other time-bound *mitzvot*, they fulfill a *mitzvah* by doing so. She should recite the blessing of *leishev basuccah* before eating, according to *Ashkenaz* custom. Those of *Sephardic* descent do not recite a blessing on time-bound *mitzvot*. The same laws apply to the *mitzvah* of the taking of the four species.

Chanukah

Women are obligated to light the *menorah* on Chanukah. Although this *mitzvah* is time-bound, they are nonetheless obligated since women were an integral part of the Chanukah miracle. A married woman or girl fulfills her obligation through the man of the household lighting the *menorah* with intent to include all those present.

Women have a custom not to sew or do laundry during the first half hour the candles are burning. It is desirable to have a more festive meal than usual throughout the days of Chanukah.

Purim

On the Shabbat preceding Purim, we read the Torah portion recounting how Amalek attacked us after our departure from Egypt. It is a positive *mitzvah* to remember the atrocities that Amalek did to the Jewish People and to obliterate his name. (Haman is a descendent of Amalek.) It is a subject of great debate whether women are included in this *mitzvah*. The prevalent practice among women is to make every effort to attend this special Torah reading. If a woman is unable to do so, she should attempt to hear the Torah reading on *Purim* day, which also makes reference to Amalek.

Women are obligated in all the *mitzvot* which are performed on Purim. Although these *mitzvot* are time-bound, similar to Chanukah, women played an integral role in the Purim miracle, thereby obligating them in the *mitzvot* of the day. This includes hearing the *megillah*, partaking in the festive Purim meal, sending food baskets to friends, and distributing gifts to the poor.

Passover

Women are obligated to perform all of the *mitzvot* of the *seder night*. As with Chanukah and Purim, women played an integral role in the redemption from Egypt, thereby obligating them in the *mitzvot* of the seder night. This includes eating the required amount of *matzot* and *marror*, drinking the four cups of wine (or grape juice), and reciting the *haggadah*.

Counting of the Omer

Commencing on the second day of Passover, there is a positive Biblical commandment to count the *omer*. We count the days in eager anticipation of the day we received the Torah, which we celebrate fifty days later on the holiday of Shavuot. Women are not obligated to perform this time-bound *mitzvah*. The prevalent custom among most women is to recite the blessing before counting. Since most women are not accustomed to praying *ma'ariv* (the evening service), it is especially important to place some form of reminder to count *sefirah* in a frequented location in the home. In some circles, women count without a blessing.

Fast Days:

Women are required to fast on all public fast days. Children should be taught to refrain from sweets and treats on these days.

Tisha B'av

The ninth day of the Hebrew month of Av is the saddest day in the Jewish calendar. All prohibitions that apply on this day apply equally to men and women. The custom is to refrain from preparing food and cleaning the home until after midday.

Listed here are the specific halachot, laws that relate to a woman's performance of time-bound mitzvot on the Festivals

Rosh Chodesh:

A Festival for Women

Rosh Chodesh - Time of Renewal

While every festival is commanded to all segments of the Jewish nation, men and women alike, the Midrash attaches particular significance to the celebration of Rosh Chodesh for women.

The first day, or in some instances two days, of the Hebrew (lunar) month is called Rosh Chodesh, the beginning of the new month. The *mitzvah* to sanctify the new month was the first one given to the Jews as a nation, commanded by Moses to the Jews while yet in Egypt. "This month is for you, the beginnings of the months, the first it shall be for you of the months of the year" (*Exodus* 12:2). While every festival is commanded to all segments of the Jewish nation, men and women alike, the *Midrash* attaches particular significance to the celebration of *Rosh Chodesh* for women.

In Jewish law, Sabbaths and holidays are different from weekdays in regard to creative activities (מְלָאכוֹת), which are forbidden on the former and permitted on the latter. Writing, building, weaving and the like, the 39 principal categories of creative activity employed in the Tabernacle are prototypes of those actions forbidden on Sabbath and holidays. Furthermore, in the Tabernacle and the Holy Temple, special sacrifices were offered on the Sabbath and festivals, in addition to the routine daily offerings.

There are some aspects of *Rosh Chodesh*, the first day of the new month which are similar to an ordinary weekday, while other features set it apart as a quasi-holiday. The *mussaf* offering, a communal sacrifice was brought on *Rosh Chodesh* (*Numbers* 28: 11-13), and the liturgy refers to it as "a time of atonement for all their (the people of Israel's) descendants." Additionally, an abridged form of Hallel is recited on *Rosh Chodesh*, because of its semi-festival status. The Talmud (*Arachin* 10b) indicates that Hallel is recited to mark a festival, such as Passover, Shavuot and Succot, or to commemorate a miracle, such as Chanukah. The Rabbis decreed that on *Rosh Chodesh* we recite Hallel because the Torah accords it special status regarding sacrificial offerings, but in a shortened format because it does not fit the Talmud's criteria of the for the complete version.

Rosh Chodesh –
A Festival for Women

The Jerusalem Talmud (*Pesachim* 4:1) lists the custom of women not to do "work" on *Rosh Chodesh* as a proper one. Obviously, perpetuating such a custom was seen as favorable by the Rabbis, and is found in *Shulchan Aruch*, the Code of Jewish Law (*Orach Chayim* 417:1). The common practice is for women to refrain from sewing on *Rosh Chodesh* (*Tashbatz*, volume III, chapter 245), while cooking, baking and all other activities prohibited on Shabbat, are permitted.

Pirkei d'Rabbi Eliezer, attributed to the *Tanna* Rabbi Eliezer ben Horkanos, traces the significance of *Rosh Chodesh* specifically for women. When the Jews in the wilderness saw that Moses had not returned from Heaven and sought an intermediary in their service to G-d, they implored Aaron to create the golden calf. To delay the process until Moses could return, he asked the Jewish males to give him the earrings of their wives and children. "If I would ask the men to give their own ornaments," Aaron reasoned, "they would give it without delay." By asking the men to have the women and children give their jewelry, he hoped that they would refuse, thereby negating the plan. The women did in fact refuse, but not because they were reluctant to part with their jewelry.

The women told their husbands, "We will not listen to you to give our jewelry to make something which is detestable and abominable, and has no power to save us!"

Pirkei d'Rabbi Eliezer outlines the reward that women were given for their staunch refusal. G-d gave them a reward in this world — they observe *Rosh Chodesh* more fully than their male counterparts. He also gave them a reward in the World to Come — in the future they will be renewed like the new moon.

Ultimately, when the men realized that their wives would not give of their jewelry, they gave their own. Those who had adopted the practice of the Egyptians and Arabs and wore earrings, gave them to Aaron and he fashioned the golden calf.

Items used for their personal beautification, those which helped perpetuate a new generation of children to guarantee the survival of our people, were to be consecrated in the service of the Tabernacle.

The Faith of Women

The festival-like quality of *Rosh Chodesh*, when women accepted upon themselves the stringency of refraining from certain work, was a reward for their faith. What is the correlation between the refusal to part with gold and silver and the celebration of *Rosh Chodesh*? In truth, their ornaments did play a role when the Tabernacle was being built. The *kiyor*, the copper washbasin, was made from the mirrors that the women of that era graciously gave as a donation to help erect the structure which served as a repository for the Divine Presence. Items used for their personal beautification, those which helped perpetuate a new generation of children to guarantee the survival of our people, were to be consecrated in the service of the Tabernacle.

If we merit to see G-d's actions in this world, we see that reward and retribution are often given measure for measure. Our actions on earth beget a corresponding heavenly response. The actions of those women in the wilderness took mundane, ornamental objects and consecrated them for a higher purpose; G-d reciprocated their gracious and noble gift. He took an ordinary day, which had no festive overtones, sanctified it as a semi-holiday, and gave it to women as a gift throughout the generations.

Rosh Chodesh and Women – Times of Renewal

The Jewish people are compared to the moon (*Shemot Rabbah* 15). When we merit G-d's favor by performing His *mitzvot*, then we are compared to the moon as it becomes increasingly larger from the beginning to the middle of the month. If we don't follow His precepts, we are compared to the moon in its state of decline after the middle of the month. Each month the חֹדֶשׁ, the month, goes through a process of renewal, or חִידוּשׁ.

Historically, the Jewish nation as a whole also follows the waxing and waning pattern of the moon. There were fifteen generations from Abraham until King Solomon and fifteen generations from King Solomon until King Zidkiyahu and the destruction of the first Holy Temple. The generations which helped build our people came to a climax as a nation in the fifteenth generation, during the rule of King Solomon. After his death, our national destiny began to decline, until its lowest point during the reign of Zidkiyahu, in whose lifetime the first Holy Temple was destroyed.

From the time a young girl enters a period of physical growth and development and starts to mature, her personal cycle parallels that of the moon. At its peak, it represents a point of potential creativity, the ability to bring new life into the world. From that time onward, as the ability to renew and create life wanes, the potential life-force leaves her body in a fairly regular cycle. (Adapted from *Or Zarua,* Laws of *Rosh Chodesh.*) The gift of *Rosh Chodesh* was particularly suited for women, who can most greatly appreciate the wondrous balance of rise and decline on a personal, as well as cosmic, level.

Rosh Chodesh and Bat Mitzvah Allusions

Tur (Orach Chayim 417) compares *Rosh Chodesh,* in its role as a minor festival, with the three Torah-ordained festivals. Each of the Three *Regalim,* or festivals, correspond to one of our Patriarchs; Passover corresponds to Avraham, Shavuot parallels Yitzchok and Succot corresponds to Yaakov. The twelve months, which are also called festivals, מוֹעֲדִים, correspond to the Twelve Tribes. When the Jewish nation sinned with the golden calf, this profound parallel, which bound the twelve months and the Twelve Tribes, became untenable.

The women, who were not involved in donating for or worshipping the golden calf, received *Rosh Chodesh* as their reward. The twelve special days of the year became the special domain of women, to abstain from work which *halachah,* Jewish law, does not dictate as forbidden. The reward meant for the leaders of the tribes of Israel was given to their wives, and for women throughout the millennia.

As mentioned earlier, in Judaism, certain numbers are particularly significant. For example, there are seven days of the week, seven weeks from Passover till Shavuot, seven years in the *shemittah* cycle, seven *shemittah* cycles till the 50th Jubilee year, etc. The number twelve is significant, as there are twelve tribes, twelve months, twelve astrological signs. Although the

age of twelve for religious majority for a female and thirteen for a male is part of the oral tradition given to Moses at Mount Sinai (*Rosh*, Responsa 16:1), the parallel allusion of the twelve *Rosh Chodesh* months and twelve years of Bat Mitzvah is significant.

The leaders of the tribes of Israel have collective responsibility for the sins of those who worshipped and donated to the golden calf. When they were stripped of the reward inherent in each month, it was given over to the women. They were trusted with the sacred charge of adding their element of personal renewal to the *mitzvot* they were already commanded. They took upon themselves a custom to refrain from work, even though there was no Torah commandment to do so. They sanctified the mundane, and elevated the commonplace.

She is entrusted with the sacred mission of perpetuating our tradition, using her unique G-d-given talents to serve her Creator.

Such is the role of a Bat Mitzvah as she enters the ranks of Judaism as a *halachic* adult, one who accepts all the legal ramifications therein. She is entrusted with the sacred mission of perpetuating our tradition, using her unique G-d-given talents to serve her Creator. She graciously accepts the role of bearing communal responsibility, achieving a degree of maturity far beyond her twelve years. With her physical life changes as a constant reminder, she enters each month with a profound sense of renewal and commitment.

The artwork on the facing page traces the power of prayer. We thank G-d in times of joy, and beseech Him in times of adversity. We invest prayer with a power it truly has, giving it wings to ascend before the Heavenly Throne. The Jewish people are compared to a dove, and each bird is shown bearing a key. We have the means to unlock Heavenly storehouses of blessing if our prayers are propelled by heartfelt intent.

Prayer is also compared to an arrow. The harder one tugs at the bowstring, the further the arrow travels. So, too, with prayer. When one reaches into the depths of his or her soul, prayer can effectively reach its celestial destination.

לכל אשר קרוב יי
 יקראוהו באמת לכל קוראיו

Prayer:
Connecting with G-d

Prayers and Supplications

As the mainstay of the home, the Jewish woman has traditionally sought out the Guiding Hand of G-d whether to help her daily routine or direct her through difficult circumstances.

ne's potential to relate to the Al-mighty and try to understand His actions to the extent of human capability, is a privilege of the highest order. And one of the best means of accomplishing this awesome task and attaining its benefits is prayer. From Adam to Abraham, Moses to Maimonides, and until today, people have utilized this gift of prayer to beseech, to praise and to connect.

It is not surprising that the Talmud reminds us that the Torah's commandment for us to pray is expressed as *a service* of *the heart,* not of the mouth. For true prayer, whether it is the Psalms of David or the daily blessings, emanates from the deepest regions of one's heart and soul. The opportunity to ask for Divine direction is forever present. It is through this holy communication that a true spiritual relationship is formed and developed.

As the mainstay of the home, the Jewish woman has traditionally sought out the Guiding Hand of G-d whether to help her daily routine or direct her through difficult circumstances. This eternal bond is enhanced by the prayers recited and the assistance sought by every daughter of Israel.

The tear-stained, worn *Tehillim* books of countless women through the ages tell the story of their heartfelt pleas and prayers. The gates of tears are always open in Heaven. A Jewish woman can direct her sincere entreaties upward, and hopefully receive a favorable response. This, too, is Judaism's gift to the Bat Mitzvah. The key to unlock the heavenly storehouses is given to her, to channel goodness and blessing to herself, her family and the people of Israel.

Women's Obligation in Prayer

In generations past, a young girl learned the laws and customs of prayer from her mother. Today many of us are unsure of women's specific obligations in prayer and require clear guidelines. Derived from our Divine blueprint, the Torah, these guidelines have been laid out for us by our Sages.

Ramban (Nachmonides) and *Rambam* (Maimonides), the early commentaries, offer two opinions concerning a woman's obligation in prayer. According to *Rambam*, prayer is a Torah obligation, based on the verse, "You shall serve Hashem your G-d." Our Sages define "to serve" as the service of the heart, which refers to prayer. In order to fulfill one's Biblical obligation, a prayer must include the following three components: *shevach* – praise of G-d, *bakashah* – personal requests, and *hoda'ah* – thanksgiving. In addition to the Biblical obligation, the Sages instituted additional parameters, the frequency of daily prayer, the time for each prayer, and the content of each prayer. Since these rabbinic requirements are time-bound, women are not obligated to follow them. However, the basic Biblical command to recite a prayer that includes *shevach, bakashah, and hoda'ah,* applies to both men and women.

Ramban asserts that all daily prayers fall under Rabbinic decree. However, when the Sages instituted prayer, they established that all of the requirements be equally incumbent upon men and women.

As far as the practical *halachic* ruling, the *Mishnah Berurah* concludes that the *halachah* follows the opinion of the *Ramban.* Consequently women have an almost equal obligation to pray as men. The *shemoneh esrei* prayer fulfills the principal obligation of daily prayer. There are various other parts of prayer that are included in the daily obligation, as will be discussed below.

While the practice of formal daily prayer is widespread among single girls, it is less so among married women. Many women have a superseding obligation to their families, particularly when there are young children in the home. Nevertheless, many do continue to pray even after marriage to the extent that time allows. A certain amount of permitted flexibility and judgment may be required. Certainly at a point when time does allow, the resumption of the daily prayers should be of utmost priority. One should ensure that the minimum requirement for prayer (one which includes *shevach, bakashah, and hoda'ah*) be recited daily.

Morning Prayers

Modeh Ani, the first prayer of the day, expresses one's gratitude to G-d for granting another day, and should be said immediately upon arising. One should then perform the ritual hand washing, beginning with the right hand and alternating until each hand is washed three times. One should not touch any

One should pray with the awareness that she is standing before and speaking to the King of all Kings. A woman should dress as she would if going outdoors.

of the open parts of the body e.g. eyes, ears, etc. or any food items prior to washing.

Women should recite *birchot hashachar*, which includes the blessings of *al netilat yadayim, asher yotzar, elokai neshamah, birchat haTorah* and the fifteen morning blessings of thanksgiving.

Whether women are obligated to recite *pesukei d'zimrah*, the introductory chapters of prayer preceding the blessings of the *shema*, remains a subject of dispute among the *halachic* authorities. If one is able, it is certainly proper to recite the entire *pesukei d'zimrah*. Faced with limited time, one should at the minimum recite *baruch she'amar, ashrei* and *yishtabach*.

The recitation of the *shema* is a time-bound requirement, thereby exempting women. However, they should recite the *shema* and mentally concentrate on accepting G-d's Kingship upon themselves . Minimally, one should recite the actual verse of *shema yisroel*. The prevalent custom is to recite the entire three paragraphs of the *shema*. When praying without a *minyan*, (quorum of 10 men) one should preface the *shema* with the words *kel melech ne'eman*.

Women are not obligated to recite the blessings preceding the *shema*. The blessings following the *shema* should be recited since they are connected to the *shemonah esrei*. These blessings are followed by the *shemonah esrei,* the highlight and focus of all our prayers. This central prayer consists of the three abovementioned major concepts. It begins with *shevach* (praise), followed by *bakashah* (personal requests), the most lengthy section, and concludes with *hoda'ah* (thanksgiving).

Women do not customarily recite the *tachanun* prayer following *shemonah esrei*. Women are also not obligated to recite the prayer of *ashrei u'vo l'tziyon* and the *shir shel yom*. Women do generally recite the *aleinu* prayer, which concludes the three daily prayers.

Minchah

A woman's obligation to recite *minchah*, the afternoon prayer, is the same as her obligation to *daven shacharit*. She should wash her hands before beginning the *minchah* prayer.

Ma'ariv

The Sages originally instituted *Ma'ariv,* the evening prayer, as voluntary. Subsequently, men accepted it upon themselves as an obligation. For women, however, it remains voluntary. A woman who wishes to begin praying *ma'ariv* should state she is doing so *bli neder* (without a vow) so that her commitment should not take on the force of a vow. (Generally when one performs a *mitzvah* three times without mentioning *bli neder* this takes on the force of a vow.) If one did not mention *bli neder* and then wishes to desist from praying *ma'ariv*, she should consult with a rabbinic authority as to whether an annulment of vows is necessary.

Additional Laws on Prayer

Preferably one should pray *shacharit* before four hours into the day. An hour is defined as one-twelfth of the time between sunrise and sunset. If that time has passed, one can pray until midday (six hours into the day). If one missed midday, she should recite the *shemonah esrei* of *minchah* twice to substitute for the missed prayer.

Before morning prayers, one should not eat or drink (excluding water, coffee, or tea), unless for medicinal purposes. One who feels weak and lacks the strength to pray properly may eat or drink. Many *halachic* authorities note that the common custom for women is to first recite a short prayer fulfilling the basic obligation of prayer according to the *Rambam* mentioned above, and this would suffice to allow them to eat or drink.

One should not involve oneself in work before praying in the morning. This would include sorting laundry, washing dishes, cleaning, ironing, cooking, and shopping. One may perform trivial activities, such as turning on a washing machine. Work done for the purpose of a *mitzvah* also may be done. This would include shopping for Shabbos, preparing food for one's children and driving them to school.

One should pray with the awareness that she is standing before and speaking to the King of all Kings. A woman should dress as she would if going outdoors. Therefore, one should not pray wearing pajamas or slippers, unless ill.

One should choose a set place for prayer even when praying at home, and avoid praying in front of pictures of people, unless they are above eye level. Left with no alternative, one may close her eyes. A person may not pray in front of a mirror even with one's eyes closed.

Hallel

Women are generally exempt from reciting Hallel since it is a time-based *mitzvah*. However, they should recite Hallel at the Passover Seder with the other *mitzvot* of the seder (see below). Whether one is required to recite Hallel on Chanukah is a dispute among various *halachic* authorities. One should recite Hallel if she is able to do so.

Children
Praying for Parents

We pray to G-d and we pray for our parents, and hopefully our personal prayers will be answered for a life of good health, happiness and success.

ow many prayers are said by parents for their children from the day they are born until the time they grow and mature? In Judaism, the prayers start before a child is born — and continue throughout his or her lifetime! Before the child is born, parents pray to G-d that they will indeed be blessed with healthy, normal children.

Once they are born we pray for their normal development, success in their endeavors, that they be positively influenced by those around them and protected from harm, and the list goes on. As they grow, we pray that they will be upstanding people, well-mannered, well-behaved, healthy young adults. But we don't stop praying. Will they maintain the legacy of past generations to help build their future?

There are three partners in a person: G-d, one's father and one's mother (Talmud, *Kiddushin* 30b). The physical properties and characteristics are given to us by our parents. Have you ever been told, "You have your mother's smile or your father's beautiful eyes?" Your soul, your essence, what makes you unique, is G-d's gift to you.

A partnership needs cooperation and teamwork to succeed. Each one is concerned with the success of his or her partner, because their success is our success. G-d wants all of His children to succeed in life. Everything we go through in life is ultimately for our own benefit, though sometimes it is difficult for us to understand. Parents pray for their children, as they help forge another link in the family chain, and carry on the eternity of our people.

And children have to pray for parents, as we all need those important partners in life. They are our teachers, our role models, guides, sounding boards, sources of joy and of comfort, and so much more. Even if there are times when we don't see things exactly as they do, they are crucial to our existence and well-being. We pray to G-d and we pray for our parents, and hopefully our personal prayers will be answered for a life of good health, happiness and success.

וְהֵשִׁיב לֵב אָבוֹת עַל בָּנִים וְלֵב בָּנִים עַל אֲבוֹתָם

A Child's Prayer

May it be your will Hashem our G-d and G-d of our forefathers, that our father, mother and we should be strong and healthy to truly serve you. Shower upon them and upon us an abundant livelihood, much success and goodness to enable us to serve you in truth and happiness.

Instill in our hearts the will to listen to our parents and enable us to honor them as you desire. May our father and mother raise us for Torah, chupah and good deeds. May they be healthy and successful in all of their endeavors with the resources to provide for all of our needs graciously. Fulfill all the requests of our hearts for goodness.

Our father in heaven save us with all of Israel, and may we merit to glorify the honor of your great name and the honor of the Torah always. May the words of my mouth and the thoughts of my heart find favor before you, my rock and redeemer.

יְהִי רָצוֹן מִלְּפָנֶיךָ יְיָ אֱלֹהֵינוּ וֵאלֹהֵי אֲבוֹתֵינוּ שֶׁיִּהְיוּ אָבִינוּ וְאִמֵּנוּ וַאֲנַחְנוּ בְּרִיאִים וַחֲזָקִים לַעֲבֹד אוֹתְךָ בֶּאֱמֶת. וְתַשְׁפִּיעַ לָהֶם וְלָנוּ פַּרְנָסָה בִּרְוַח וְהַצְלָחָה מְרֻבָּה וְכָל טוּב לַעֲבֹד אוֹתְךָ בֶּאֱמֶת וּבְשִׂמְחָה.

וְתֵן בְּלִבֵּנוּ לִשְׁמֹעַ בְּקוֹל אָבִינוּ וְאִמֵּנוּ. וְהוֹשִׁיעֵנוּ שֶׁנְּכַבֵּד אוֹתָם תָּמִיד כַּאֲשֶׁר רְצוֹנְךָ הַטּוֹב עָלֵינוּ. וְנַעֲבֹד אוֹתְךָ בֶּאֱמֶת וְיִגְדְּלוּ אָבִינוּ וְאִמֵּנוּ אוֹתָנוּ לְתוֹרָה וּלְחֻפָּה וּלְמַעֲשִׂים טוֹבִים. וְיִהְיוּ מֻצְלָחִים בַּבְּרִיאוּת וְכָל טוּב וַעֲשִׁירוּת לִתֵּן לָנוּ מוֹהַר וּמַהֵן וְכָל טוּב בְּסֵבֶר פָּנִים יָפוֹת. וּתְמַלֵּא כָּל מִשְׁאֲלוֹת לִבֵּנוּ לְטוֹבָה.

אָבִינוּ שֶׁבַּשָּׁמַיִם הוֹשִׁיעֵנוּ כָּל זֶה בִּכְלַל כָּל יִשְׂרָאֵל. וְנִזְכֶּה לְהַגְדִּיל כְּבוֹד שִׁמְךָ הַגָּדוֹל וּכְבוֹד תּוֹרָתְךָ תָּמִיד. יִהְיוּ לְרָצוֹן אִמְרֵי פִי וְהֶגְיוֹן לִבִּי לְפָנֶיךָ יְיָ צוּרִי וְגוֹאֲלִי:

סֵפֶר שַׁעֲרֵי צִיּוֹן

Honor your father and mother — כבד את אביך ואת אמך

Portraits of Greatness:

Inspiring Stories About Young Women Like You

Portraits of Greatness

e are all used to reading biographies of great people, individuals who are uniquely gifted by the Almighty with talents, skills or personalities that set them apart from their peers. In Jewish history, we stand in awe of how much they achieved during their lifetimes. These great men and women were leaders of their respective generations, and we humbly acknowledge how exalted they were — and how it is hard for us to even measure up to their standards.

Rav Yitzchok Hutner ז"ל (1906–1980), revered head of Yeshivat Rabbeinu Chaim Berlin in New York, offers a fascinating insight into how we view these great individuals. In his collection of Letters and Writings (Letter 128), he writes to a student who was struggling with personal shortcomings in his quest for spiritual growth. "We often tend to view these great people as finished products," says Rav Hutner. "The great *Chofetz Chaim* is revered as a leader of the Jewish people, noted for disseminating the laws of *lashon hara*, forbidden speech and gossip. The piety of this great sage is legendary, but what about all the years of internal struggle *until he became* the *Chofetz Chaim*? There were periods in his life when he had to overcome a negative tendency, or work to perfect his character as he was developing. One should look at these great people as role models in their period of struggle and growth, as *that* is a lesson from which we all can learn."

Rav Moshe Feinstein ז"ל (1895–1986), noted *halachic* authority and leader of the past generation, makes a similar observation about a statement found in our morning prayers.

אָבִינוּ אָב הָרַחֲמָן הַמְרַחֵם רַחֵם עָלֵינוּ וְתֵן בְּלִבֵּנוּ לְהָבִין וּלְהַשְׂכִּיל לִשְׁמֹעַ לִלְמֹד וּלְלַמֵּד לִשְׁמֹר וְלַעֲשׂוֹת וּלְקַיֵּם אֶת כָּל דִּבְרֵי תַלְמוּד תּוֹרָתֶךָ בְּאַהֲבָה.

Our Father, merciful Father, who acts with mercy, have mercy upon us, implant in our hearts (the ability) to understand and elucidate, to listen, to learn, to teach, to safeguard, to perform and to fulfill all of the words of Your Torah's teachings, with love.

The requests we have of the Almighty are great and varied. We seek His Divine assistance in becoming better people by grasping the profound nature and teachings of His Torah. We beseech

Him in learning and in doing. We realize that all of us have the potential to *learn* His Torah — but isn't it presumptuous of us to ask God to be a *teacher* of His torah? Even when one keeps the *mitzvot*, can the accountant, doctor, housewife, student or plumber feel that they can adequately teach God's Torah?

Rav Moshe ז״ל says that indeed, every person is a teacher of Torah and God's lessons for living. Even those who don't teach in a classroom are always teaching by example. When we are kind and compassionate, humble and giving, we are emulating the ways of our Creator and sharing profound lessons with those we meet. Does the way I speak, dress, pray and act reflect the teachings of Torah, or do I exhibit behavior that is less than admirable? My peers are watching me, whether I am aware of it or not, and learning from my positive — and unfortunately sometimes from my negative — behavior. We pray to God, "enable me to learn and to understand, and to be a teacher and positive role model for all those I meet."

Roles and Role Models

The following collection of inspiring stories is somewhat unique. Other sections of this volume have dealt with some of the most noted heroines of Jewish history, our Matriarchs and women of the Bible. Certainly they have much to share about the character needed to help build our nation. "But I couldn't do that!" you protest. "I live in the 21st century. They were different, the times were different, life was different! Can God possibly expect *me* to be like them?"

The answer is, of course not. We look at great people to see the ultimate potential of noble individuals, and see how it can possibly relate to our world and our times. The stories to follow are about young women — just like you. Most of these young ladies are around Bat Mitzvah age, and we can nonetheless call them our teachers. By their courage, their sensitivity and their *midot*, character, they have shown what growing to be a *Bat Yisrael* is all about. They may be young in age, but mature beyond their tender years. They have demonstrated by their example how noble a Jewish spirit can be, and hopefully, we will come along to learn from their experiences.

Special thanks to Mrs. Bayla Sheva Brenner who helped compile these stories, conduct interviews and masterfully craft them into inspiring messages from which we can all benefit. Each of us has a unique ability and special role, and we can all learn from these gifted "teachers" and superb role models.

Everyone in our class knew Penina* came from an unstable home. It was, unfortunately, all too obvious. With her acne-ridden cheeks, obesity, and lack of social graces, she wore her young life's problems for all to view. Academics were not her forte either. We all cringed when she was called on in class. Over the years, she never knew the answers, yet it seemed to hurt her just as deeply every time. None of the girls tried to befriend her. No one wanted to get entangled in her quagmire of misery. I guess we were afraid we'd never get out. But not Judith. She wasn't afraid.

Shayna was the first to notice the change. "Look at Penina," as she nudged me in the ribs. "There's something different about her. What is it?"

"What do you mean?"

"Take a good look. I know there's something, something." I studied Penina's face and realized right away what Shayna was trying to get at. Her cheeks were clear, actually smooth and soft looking. Almost feminine. Almost pretty. That was the first change. I started keeping an eye on her. As the months passed, I noticed Penina had a new lightness in her step.

"Shayn? Do you think Penina's losing weight?"

"Yup. Check out her hair too." I did. It went from frizz to sleek and sheen.

"She must have had it relaxed, right?" I asked.

"Yup. For sure."

"What do you think is going on?"

"I don't know, but it's wonderful. A miracle!" During the next fall, I remarked at how she began to look people in the eyes when she talked, instead of staring uneasily at her feet. She actually initiated conversations with newfound warmth and confidence.

The peak of the transformation happened in the middle of *Chumash* class. Mrs. Nussbaum directed a really tough

---

*All names have been changed.

question from *Sefer Vayikra* straight at Penina. She hesitated, as she always did, but then she cleared her throat and slowly, articulately gave the right answer.

"Excellent!" proclaimed Mrs. Nussbaum, trying to contain her delight. When all eyes finally lifted their surprised gaze away from her, she let go a smile of such profound joy, that my heart leapt for her.

Through the remainder of high school, Penina no longer dragged along on the periphery of life. She had become an integral part of a lovely circle of friends. One that embraced her, appreciated her, and would now be incomplete without her. Her school performance improved year after year, culminating with her graduating near the top of our class. I lost track of her after high school and recently heard she married a special young man and has built a truly happy Jewish home.

I'm sure the other girls wondered, as I did, how this broken girl transformed into a confident, self-possessed young woman. No one spoke much about it, but I think they suspected Judith was behind it. I'm sure she was. I could tell by the way they connected when together. I sensed a mutual admiration, the way sisters feel. It was Judith's group of friends that Penina became a part of. I know she saw the person she was meant to be, beyond the scars.

While we chose to watch from afar, afraid to get too close to the damage, Judith understood the essence of *ahavat Yisrael,* love of a fellow Jew. It means first feeling another person's pain, then seeing the potential, and most importantly, helping in every way to reach it. It was she who befriended Penina, went with her to a dermatologist, found a support group for compulsive overeaters, shopped for clothes with her, tutored her, welcomed her into her circle of friends, and helped her believe in her unique and infinite value as a *bat Yisrael.*

I regret that I didn't help Penina, but there are many Penina's around us, who await a kind word, a caring gesture, our friendship.

᪥   ᪥   ᪥

As told by Mrs. Chana Klein, teacher at
Rachel Dwek Bet Yaakob, Deal, New Jersey

I had come there to inspire Jewish souls, but I felt myself inspired – by their fiery enthusiasm and by their amazing stories.

A Young Girl From Lodz Finds Her Way Back

I recently stood witness to the spiritual renaissance among today's youth in Eastern Europe. I was asked to invest a week with these teenagers, introducing them to the beauty of Torah and *mitzvot,* at a special retreat two hours from Cracow. I flew in from New York, traveling a full day to reach the resort. The hall buzzed with excitement, as the participants huddled around me, asking question after question, their souls impatient for answers.

All the participants experienced inspiring days filled with lectures and electrifying davening. They couldn't wait to hear more, grasping each *mitzvah* as a newfound opportunity – one they never imagined they would possess. Most were not observant, yet a sense of complete Torah commitment permeated the resort each day. I had come there to inspire Jewish souls, but I felt myself inspired – by their fiery enthusiasm and by their amazing stories.

On the final morning of the program, I bid the participants a heartfelt farewell. As I quickly descended the stage, rushing to make it to Cracow in time to catch the next train to the airport, a young girl stopped me.

"Rabbi," she said. "I have to talk to you about something important, but I can't talk here."

Her serious manner made an impression, and I guided her toward a conference room.

"I was raised as a Catholic. All my life I attended church each Sunday. I did everything my friends did. And, like them, I never thought much about my ancestors. Then my grandmother passed away. She had lived with us for as long as I could remember. I was very close to my *babushka*. Both my mother and I deeply mourned her passing."

"One day, the postman delivered an envelope with my grandmother's death certificate. I studied the document. It seemed they had sent us someone else's papers. I ran to my mother, and told her that we would have to apply for a new certificate."

"'Why?'" she asked. 'What's wrong with this one?'"

"They sent us someone else's," I said. 'This document is for somebody named Miriam Reinman'."

"My mother's jaw dropped and she began to weep. I couldn't calm her. She looked up and said, 'There is no mistake. *Babushka's* name was Miriam Reinman, just like it is written. Lena, I don't know how to tell you this, but your grandmother was Jewish. I am Jewish too.' Then my mother looked straight into my eyes. 'And so are you.'"

"I felt like I had been hit by lightening. I had never hated Jews, like some of my friends, but I was entrenched in my Catholic way of life."

"My parents lived through the Holocaust," said my mother. "'After all they had seen and went through, they made a decision that their children would not suffer as they had. They would hide their identity forever, to spare their family from persecution. So, they raised me as a Catholic. I knew their secret, but I kept it from you.'"

"I went outside to try to absorb what I had just learned. I wandered about the streets, trying to sort out my thoughts and feelings. Suddenly, I noticed a group of teenagers carrying suitcases. They were lining up in front of a bus. I recognized one of my classmates and asked her where she was going."

"'I'm going to a retreat to learn about Judaism.'"

"I asked her to tell more details about the trip. When I walked away, I imagined my hometown, Lodz, 70 years back, bustling with Jewish men, women, and children. I could almost hear the echo of their prayers. For days I toyed with the idea of joining my friend. I could not find peace knowing not far away, there was a gathering going on that could answer my deepest questions. I decided to come. At first I was a curious observer, but these few days have changed me. You answered many questions, but now I have the biggest one of all. Rabbis are supposed to know the secrets of Heaven and earth. How about giving an answer to a 15-year-old Jewish girl from Lodz?"

"You already have your answer," I said. "You can't go back to your old way of life – your soul won't let you. Your world has been rocked. Your life will never be the same again. You need to learn about Judaism, to find out everything you can about Torah and *mitzvos*."

Lena lowered her eyes and sobbed.

"I understand, Rabbi," she said through her tears. "But I really don't know if I have the strength."

"Lena," I said. "You'll have the strength. Heaven is helping you already. Your grandmother is helping you. Her death

certificate was a sign from Above, delivered directly into your hands. It is a sign that she feels responsible for your spiritual welfare. I believe that you will be successful in your search."

Lena left the retreat, resolute in her plan to learn more. She signed up for a Jewish study program and began her journey back to Torah and Judaism. I am sure that her *babushka*, Miriam, is smiling down at her granddaughter, who with determination and joy, reclaimed a heritage almost lost to her and proudly rejoined the Jewish People.

&. &. &.

As told by Rabbi Dovid Goldwasser, Rav, Kehillas Bais Yitzchok, and noted author and lecturer.

Cultivating a Diamond

Mrs. Lewin* checked the clock on her dresser then checked her appearance in the mirror. PTA night. What was she so nervous about? As she walked quickly down the upstairs hallway, she decided to turn back. She didn't want to leave without saying a few words to her daughter, who might be a bit anxious about tonight as well. She found Sarah curled up cozy on her bed, leafing through a clothing catalog.

"See you, Sarah. I'm on my way."

"Send my regards to Mrs. Klein," she grinned the grin I've come to love – a soft lift of her freckled cheeks revealing the comfortable confidence within. I've worked diligently to cultivate that sense of herself, monitoring constantly. I repeat my parental mantra throughout our precious twelve years together, "Be generous with praise. Edit unnecessary criticism." Not an easy feat. Talk about controlling oneself! But it can be done and the payoff is gratifying beyond words. Time to go; Mrs. Klein awaits Sarah's Ima.

"Mrs. Lewin, so nice to see you. Please have a seat."

She looked particularly put together this evening. It must be unnerving, not to mention intimidating, having to wow understandably demanding parents with the intelligence, grace, and compassionate authority they expect of a teacher.

I repeat my parental mantra throughout our precious twelve years together, "Be generous with praise. Edit unnecessary criticism." Not an easy feat.

---

*All names have been changed.

"Let me tell you about your daughter," she cleared her throat.

"Please, let *me* tell you about my daughter," I smiled politely and continued. "Let me tell you of the things you may not know about Sarah."

"Sure. Why not? Please, go ahead."

"Her brother, who attends HASC, a school for seriously disabled children, has seizures every night and needs oxygen every morning. He requires help getting dressed, regular diaper changes, and a good hour getting him ready to go to school. Our family is up with him on and off through most nights. One Monday last month, Sarah and I both had a vacation day. My son didn't, so I set the alarm as usual and got up early to take care of his needs. There by his side Sarah was changing his diaper and telling him what a wonderful day he was going to have at school."

"Ima, it's your day off. Don't worry, I'll take care of Moshe," I attempted to take over, but Sarah wouldn't let me.

"It's your vacation day! Enjoy it. Go back to sleep. We're fine, aren't we Moishele?" She gave him a kiss full of love and shooed me away.

"You are such a source of pride and joy for me. Did you know that?"

"Yeah. Yeah," she smiled that smile that I love.

"I went back to the bedroom with a most grateful lump in my throat. Be generous with praise. Edit unnecessary criticism. It's a phrase I tell myself for the benefit of the children and the people I hope that they'll grow to be."

"Thank you for giving me a deeper glimpse into Sarah," said Mrs. Klein. "Also for the salient advice. Something teachers need to keep in mind as well."

"Now, tell me, how's she doing?" I asked.

"Mrs. Lewin, I think you said it all."

🐝 🐝 🐝

As told by Mrs. Rina Malinowitz,
Principal, Rachel Dwek Bet Yaakob, Deal, New Jersey.

Rose stood near her father on the dock of a Polish harbor with a steamer trunk and the sadness of separation between them. Her parents chose their little Rose, mature beyond her twelve years, to venture out to America. Their life in Poland was wrought with daily hardship and hunger. Yet, after scrimping and saving, her family collected enough for a one-way ticket that would transport their young daughter to a better life in " the golden land". That was their hope.

Her father lifted the trunk and walked silently towards the ship, carrying a lifetime of sorrow and pride. He lowered the trunk onto the deck and turned to his daughter's innocent young face. He wanted only to gather her into his arms and carry her back home, but instead told her, "Rose, *mein kinde* (my child), remember always, God in Heaven is watching over you wherever you go. Keep His holy laws. Never forget that more than the Jews have kept the Shabbos, the Shabbos has kept the Jews. Rose, don't ever forget who you are."

"Tatte! Tatte!" Rose locked her arms around the waist of her father's overcoat, pushing her face into his chest and sobbed. The ship's blast signaled the imminent departure. He hugged her with all his might and turned and walked down the gangplank.

Rose looked out at the ocean, as vast and dark as the uncertainty welling inside her. Would her relatives in America take her in with warmth and kindness? She feared the loneliness she would have to face each day without her loved ones. One day swirled into the next and at last the ship entered New York harbor. The passengers clamored against the railing, shouting and clapping, eager to enter the new land of freedom and prosperity. Rose stood stone still, quiet and contained in her insecurity, surrounded by air she had never breathed.

Her relatives waved excitedly as she stepped off the ship pointing towards New York's jagged gray skyline. They called her their "greenhorn" cousin.

Before long she became part of the family and found a job as a sewing machine operator. The stark differences between her old home and America jostled her senses. Jewish immigrants shed much of their lives before: their modesty, keeping the

Yet, after scrimping and saving, her family collected enough for a one-way ticket that would transport their young daughter to a better life in " the golden land". That was their hope.

laws of kashrus, and observing the Shabbos. Rose's relatives told her they had no need for the "old-fashioned" religious practices. "We're in America now!" Rose couldn't forget her father's words. She wore the pretty new clothes her relatives gave her, and a fashionable new hair cut, but held tight to her determination to keep Shabbos.

Every week, Rose gave her boss a new excuse for her absence on Saturdays. One week her tooth ached, another it was her stomach. After a few weeks, the foreman called her over. "I like your work, Rose. And I like you. But you have to stop with this Shabbos business. Either you come in this Saturday, or you can just find yourself another job."

Rose's relatives pleaded with her to work on Shabbos, that in America, it was a must. She wanted to appease them, but her father's words kept ringing in her ears. She felt inextricably caught between two worlds.

The week passed and Rose didn't know what she would do. Her *tatte* wasn't there to help her be strong. She wanted the approval of her relatives who treated her with such kindness and generosity. Rose longed for friends and to fit into this new life. "Rose sweetheart, listen to us. It's for your own good." But how can she forget Shabbos, the beauty of *Yiddishkeit* that was still so much a part of her? And her father's plea, "Don't forget who you are!"

On Friday, Rose walked to work, lost in her thoughts. She turned on her machine, listening to its hum joining the other machines. Would it be so awful to do this tomorrow too? She had to make a decision. She gazed out the window as the sun slowly descended over the buildings of the Lower East Side. A feeling rose from the very center of her soul. There was no question. She was a Jew and she would keep the Shabbos.

She left the house Saturday morning as though she were headed for work as usual. She walked aimlessly around the streets of Manhattan until she grew tired and sat on a bench in Tompkin's Square park. Rose watched the pigeons ruffle their feathers and bob their little round heads. And she began to sing, "*Yonah matza bo manoach…*" (On the Sabbath the dove found rest.) She remained among the pigeons, singing Shabbos songs and cried for the comfort and serenity of the Shabbos she once knew. When three stars shone in the dark sky, Rose smiled at her triumph, yet knew this victory would carry a price. She would come back to no job and an alienated family.

As her father told her,
more than the Jews
keep the Shabbos,
Shabbos keeps the Jews.

She turned the corner towards her home and heard someone screaming her name. Her cousin Joe ran towards her.

She avoided his face. "Oh, Joe, what will become of me? I kept Shabbos and lost my job. Now everyone will be angry and disappointed with me. What am I going to do? She couldn't hold back her tears.

"Rose, didn't you hear?"

"Hear what?"

"There was a terrible fire in the factory. There was no way out of the building. People jumped to their deaths. Only 40 people survived." He wept openly and continued through his tears, "Don't you see? Because you kept Shabbos, you are alive. Because of your Shabbos, you survived."

Out of 190 workers, Rose Goldstein was one of the few survivors of the infamous Triangle Shirtwaist Factory fire on Saturday, March 25, 1911, when 146 immigrant workers present at the factory lost their lives. As her father told her, more than the Jews keep the Shabbos, Shabbos keeps the Jews.

Adapted from a story in Small Miracles for the Jewish Heart, published by Adams Media Corporation, as told by Goldy Rosenberg.

Truly
at The Top of
Her Class

Rabbi Goldwasser entered his study and gently closed the door behind him. He swung his briefcase onto the leather seat of the chair beside his desk, where many have occupied, some leaning forward anxiously, others looking down shamefully, with eyes pacing to avoid the unavoidable. Nervous, distraught, wanting, all of them come to the rabbi for hope and for needed *chizuk*. As the briefcase landed, the phone rang. He lifted the receiver and quickly settled in his desk chair with a "Hello." A young girl's voice stammered and then faltered.

"This is Rabbi Goldwasser. May I help you?" Silence.

"Is there something you wanted to ask me?"

"Y...yes. But... I'm not sure how to ask." One word solidly attached to the next. She's relaxing. A good sign.

"Just start from the beginning." Silence again.

"Would it be easier if you came to see me in person?

"Okay." She meant it.

"Why don't you come to the *shul* before *mincha* tomorrow. We can talk then. Alright?"

"Alright."

A petite girl of no more than twelve years stood patiently by the rabbi's open door. "Come in!" smiled Rabbi Goldwasser and motioned for her to sit. She sat down and folded her hands in her lap.

"Tell me. What's on your mind?"

"There are 200 girls in my graduating class. I'm valedictorian." Her face contorted, the girl looked tortured.

"So, what's the question? You don't feel you deserve it?" No reply. Just agonized sighs.

"You don't have the grades for it?" Still nothing. "I can't give you an answer without a question."

"The problem is that there's another girl in our class who really wants it and doesn't do as well scholastically, but works very hard and it would mean a tremendous amount to her... Can I turn it down?"

"Maybe, but what will your parents say? It sounds like this other girl needs the encouragement. I can imagine what your sacrifice would do for her." Rabbi Goldwasser thought a moment. "This is not a *psak halacha* (Jewish legal decision). You should first ask permission from your parents. If they agree to it, then go to the school administrators and I'll step in to help you with that discussion."

Apparently relieved by the rabbi's plan, the girl stood, nodded a short but grateful thank you, and hastened out of the room.

Rabbi Goldwasser felt certain that the girl's parents would see this as a noble gesture. But on second thought, their daughter had worked so hard all her years in school. They could understandably contend that the honor was something she rightfully earned, and she shouldn't give that acknowledgement away.

Hers was the first message on the rabbi's answering machine when he arrived in his study the next day. With the same relief in her voice, she reported that her parents gave her permission to let her schoolmate experience the pride of becoming this year's valedictorian. But that's not the end of the story.

This was a school that played strictly by the rules and rarely made concessions or exceptions. Never in its history of graduating classes were there ever two valedictorians – until this year. Apparently, they too were moved by this young girl's sensitivity and valor. At an age when recognition for arduous effort plays such a vital role in a developing young woman's sense of herself, this young lady did the extraordinary. She summoned up the courage to forfeit public reward for a job well done to another, who perhaps needed it more. This valedictorian's hard-won nobility clearly reflects her parents' powerful example.

❧ ❧ ❧

As told by Rabbi Dovid Goldwasser,
Rav, Kehillas Bais Yitzchok, and noted author and lecturer.

Only God possesses the picture of the person each one of us has the potential to become. He gives us the vital tools with which to accomplish this all-important endeavor. To be sure, it is a moment-by-moment task and if we do our part, He will help us accomplish the rest as we struggle to grow, by rising to our challenges and extending ourselves towards others. Listen to the voices of these young women, each on her individual journey to becoming her best self.

Views From The Classroom

Hannah*:

Everyone feels insulted at one time or another. It's just that way with people. We're not always in the best mood and some days we seem to run up against one barrier after another; frustration builds and it takes every ounce of energy to avoid exploding with the wrong words.

I've been working hard at refraining from throwing back a nasty comment when someone says something insensitive to me. I swallow my anger and manage, with great effort, to respond in a calm and cordial way, when it would be so easy to give into the momentary satisfaction of saying something cynical.

"Do not do something abhorrent to another Jew that I would find abhorrent if done to me". That is the essence of every relationship. So I do my best to be there for a friend in the way I would want her to be there for me. I agree, although I sometimes have to bite my tongue, to do a friend a favor, especially if it isn't convenient. After all – how can it be "out of my way" when a *mitzvah* is *the way.* I let the scholastically weaker students know they are welcome to call on me if they need help with schoolwork. It's something I know I would appreciate (especially in math).

*All names have been changed.

I try to bring happiness or lighten life's load for people and it seems everyone has their own burden. On Sunday afternoons, I visit an elderly woman. She lives alone and every time she sees me, she lights up. That's when I know I couldn't be doing anything better with my Sundays.

During the summer, I go from bungalow to bungalow, inquiring if the mothers need help babysitting for their children. They eagerly accept my offer and thank me over and over again. Truth is, I feel a little uncomfortable with all the thanks, because I know I'm only trying to do what's right. It's what Hashem wants from me.

Elissa:

My parents have six children. Because I'm the oldest girl, I often baby-sit for my younger sisters and brothers when my parents attend weddings or other obligations. I've come to welcome the opportunity to help them out. I'm fortunate that I do well in school and I am often asked by the other girls to study with them or help them with homework. When I think about it, it's a privilege to be able to make a difference in their growing stronger in their skills and understanding. Last year, in the 7th grade, I listened to a particularly difficult math lesson for a few minutes and then spent the rest of the math class explaining it to three other classmates who were looking pretty panicked. They told me they didn't have a clue of what the concepts meant and called me a lifesaver.

During the summer, my friend and I noticed that all the toddlers' mothers didn't have a solid moment to relax. We're pretty good with young children and decided to organize a day camp for the pre-schoolers, which thrilled both the kids and their Moms.

Being the oldest girl, my Mom appreciates the fact that I love to bake and cook, and welcomes my assistance in the kitchen. She also gets a kick out of the fact that I want to help her bathe the younger kids and work with them on their homework. On Shabbat morning, I let my Mom sleep in and I play with my little sibs. On Shabbat afternoon, I play with the younger children on my block, supervising them so that no one gets into a fight or gets hurt.

I try to see life positively. It's not always easy, but I find it makes me happier and helps me get into the habit of seeing the good in people. It really works.

Cheryl:

I have a sixteen year-old sister with Downs Syndrome. We shared a room until my brothers went off to *yeshiva*. I always let her know how much I love her and that we'll always be close. I'm usually the one who "tucks her in" at night. Sometimes she awakens crying from bad dreams and I'm able to comfort her. In the morning, we choose the clothes she will wear for the day and fix her lunch. When my friends visit me, I try to involve her in our games. I usually place her on someone's team, so she can really feel like a participant. I know a family across our street that has two seriously handicapped children. Since I'm pretty experienced at this, I've started to visit them and play with them too.

I have to admit, when I was younger, I resented all the attention my sister got. I've worked hard to realize that I have to appreciate the fact that I'm healthy and have gotten to a point where I am truly happy for the extra attention she receives.

Batsheva:

I'm the youngest of four. People seem to think it's great being the youngest and the truth is it can be. I look up to my older sisters. I sometimes join them when they visit lonely elderly people. They've shown me the importance of helping others and I try to live up to that ideal on my own. I arranged a "phone date" with an academically weaker classmate and find I get as much out of it as she does. Maybe more.

In the summertime I work in a program for special children with mental and/or physical handicaps; I prefer to call them "challenges". I've taught them arts and crafts and even how to play baseball. During the summer nights, my friends and I go over the laws of *Shmiras Haloshon*, so that we can really know, not merely assume, what is proper to say and what is not, especially about others.

I have come to love prayer. I think it's amazing that Hashem wants to hear from every one of us, including *me*. I think it's so important to avoid conversation while the class prays. I've actually summoned up the courage to remind my friends to show the proper respect to G-d and their classmates by working harder on being quiet during services. They're still my friends. Imagine that!

As told by Mrs. Esther Kuessous, Assistant Principal,
Prospect Park Yeshiva, Brooklyn, New York

> *I sometimes join them when they visit lonely elderly people. They've shown me the importance of helping others and I try to live up to that ideal on my own.*

ummer camp, a carefree suspension of time filled with activity and sun, that is, unless it rains. The sky turns gray, campers complain, and counselors panic. But as with every situation life brings, it's what we do with the given situation that determines the quality of each day, not the weather.

One August day in 1995, the heavens opened and the rain poured down upon the Catskill Mountains of New York State. The 11-year-old girls of Bunk 3 of the Junior Division of Camp Kayitz* had a serious case of cabin fever. The third rainy day in less than a week, and they had reached a frenzied state. Another thunderclap. "Oh no, more rain!" the bunk screamed in unison. The two teenaged counselors, Shoshana Bloom* and Rina Erenreich, locked eyes in a mutual moment of exasperation.

"If we have another water fight, like the one on Monday, I think I'm going to quit this job," informed her co-counselor.

Rina, the practical one of the two, leaped off her bed and announced, "If any of you have a bathing suit on the line, you'd better bring it in." Twelve girls went for the door and ran out into the downpour. About a half a minute later, they returned drenched and laughing. Exhilarated from the run, Zissy yelled, "Let's see who can jump up and reach the light bulb!"

"Not so fast, Zissy," Rina cautioned, as she dodged the dripping bathing suits hanging over the rafters. "That might be the safest thing to do." Rina reached for her poncho and threw it over her head.

"Where are you going?" asked Shoshana afraid of the imminent abandonment.

"I'm running over the the social hall to see if we can use it for a game of *machanayim*."

Within minutes she returned, soaked and dejected.

"Another bunk beat us to it?" asked Shoshana. Rina rolled her eyes and nodded.

"Do you have any idea what we can do with these kids today?" Shoshana pleaded.

---

*All names have been changed.

"How about the family dining room? Did you check to see if it was empty?"

"Taken. Mrs. Chayal is using it for one of her C.P.R. classes."

"But she probably doesn't need the whole room," Rina thought out loud. "Maybe we could use part of it."

"Apparently you don't know Mrs. Chayal very well. She insists on absolute quiet during those classes. I remember when I was a camper and took C.P.R. with her. She wouldn't stand for even the slightest disturbance. Trust me, she'd never allow our bunk to play in there."

"I've got an idea," said Shoshana suddenly hopeful. "Why don't we ask Mrs. Chayal if our bunk can observe her C.P.R. class?" If they promise to keep absolutely quiet, maybe she'll agree."

"It's definitely worth a shot. I'll go back and ask her. I don't mind going out again. I'm soaked already. Maybe if I explain just how desperate we are to find something to occupy our bunk, she'll take pity on us," Rina smiled.

As Rina entered the large room, she heard nothing but the clear voice of Mrs. Sterna Chayal, the camp nurse. She tried to creep in without a sound, but the squishing of her wet sneakers gave her away. She approached the nurse and asked her with all the politeness she could muster.

"I'm sorry," came the reply. "I think New York State law requires that no one under the age of 14 is allowed to take C.P.R. The girls in Bunk 3 are three years shy of that."

"I'm not asking for you to teach them," Rina explained. "I'm only asking if you'll let them watch your class just for today. They are bored out of their minds after three days of nonstop rain. If Shoshana and I assure you that they won't make a peep, would you please let them watch?" She swallowed hard and waited. Mrs. Chayal relented.

The counselors instructed the excited campers to tiptoe over the back row of the C.P.R. class. Mrs. Chayal had just finished her introduction to cardiopulmonary resuscitation and began demonstrating how to apply the appropriate maneuver to save a choking infant. Not a bored camper in sight, the girls sat completely enthralled by the lesson. At the close of the class, Rina and Shoshana thanked Mrs. Chayal on behalf of their bunk and brought the girls back to *daven mincha* and get ready for supper.

Five months after camp had long ended, on a bitter cold winter evening, Sterna Chayal received a phone call from Mrs.

As Rina entered the large room, she heard nothing but the clear voice of Mrs. Sterna Chayal, the camp nurse.

Tova Sherman, whose daughter, Zissy, was in Bunk 3 during that summer. She called to express her profound gratitude and to relate a frightening episode that had taken place earlier in the week at their home.

The Shermans were sitting around the dinner table after a hectic day. Dinner was ready, the older children finished their homework early, and Yaakov Sherman arrived home well before he usually did. Mrs. Sherman suddenly noticed her 10-month-old, Duvi's face turned blue. She scooped him up and screamed, "Quick, call Hatzolah!" Yaakov ran to his wife, stared at his baby son, and froze from panic. The other children also ran to see what happened.

"Call Hatzolah! Call Hatzolah!" Mrs. Sherman kept screaming, tears streaming now. Her husband ran to the phone. In the midst of the commotion, Zissy asked, "Why don't you try the choking infant maneuver on Duvi?"

"I've never heard of such a maneuver," shouted her panic-stricken mother.

"But I have," said Zissy.

"Then do it!" her mother cried.

The 11-year-old girl took her baby brother in her arms and with the heel of her hand delivered five sharp blows to his upper back, counting each one out loud. Then she quickly turned him around and pushed her forefinger and middle finger into his upper chest five times, again counting. The Sherman family stood mesmerized.

After banging on Duvi's back and pushing on his chest, Zissy repeated the procedure. Abruptly, everyone heard a soft gurgling sound, followed by a cough. A penny flew out of Duvi's mouth and rolled across the floor. He took a deep breath, let out a piercing wail and his natural color returned immediately. Sighs of joy, relief, and gratitude to Hashem replaced the terror. Mrs. Sherman dried her tears and turned lovingly to her daughter. "Where in the world did you learn to do that?"

Zissy explained what had happened that rainy week at summer camp and how she just "happened" to learn about the proper maneuver for saving choking infants.

Six weeks later, Mrs. Chayal received a call from Mrs. Bracha Lerner, another mother of a Camp Kayitz camper from Bunk 3. She called to thank her. Her daughter, Chanie, had been babysitting for her neighbors' children the night before. The infant son began to choke. His brothers and sisters came

running to Chanie hysterical. She walked over to the wiggling, blue infant and picked him up. She went through the proper procedure for saving a choking infant. Seconds later he spit out a small piece of Lego.

Later that night, Mrs. Lerner heard how her daughter saved the life of their neighbor's baby and how Chanie had spent a rainy afternoon that previous summer learning C.P.R. Mrs. Lerner called Mrs. Chayal the next day to tell her what resulted from one hour of one of her C.P.R. classes. Mrs. Lerner didn't know that Mrs. Sherman had also called Mrs. Chayal, a few weeks earlier to give her similar life-giving dividends for her one-hour investment.

"Thank you so much for calling," said Mrs. Chayal. "It was so thoughtful of you to tell me what happened. You should be very proud of your daughter. It takes a lot of courage and confidence for such a young girl to respond so well to such an emergency."

"Mrs. Chayal, it is I who must thank you for allowing the girls from my daughter's bunk sit in on your class. If not for that, my story might have had a very different ending."

Adapted from Zorei'a Tzedakos, by Dr. Meir Wikler, published by Feldheim Publishers

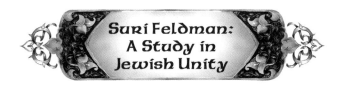

The most extraordinary thing about Suri Feldman's rescue was not the poignant story of a child lost for 48 hours in the Connecticut woods, but the compelling drama of the people drawn together to find her.

The most extraordinary thing about Suri Feldman's rescue was not the poignant story of a child lost for 48 hours in the Connecticut woods, but the compelling drama of the people drawn together to find her.

n Wednesday, May 4th 1994, during a school field trip, Suri Feldman, a slight 14-year-old Chassidic girl from Brooklyn got lost in a Connecticut forest. Alone in the dense silence, she took walks by day, rationed the food she had volunteered to hold in her knapsack for some of her school-mates, slept in the wet, black night, and prayed – unaware of the enormous outpouring of concern her crisis was generating among Jews and non-Jews.

The story of a lost child doesn't often make national news headlines. It's a tragedy with which we've become all too familiar. And yet, the disappearance of this young girl, stirred thousands of rescuers to action. The 48-hour search for Suri Feldman became one of the most extraordinary expressions of Jewish unity, and unity between Jew and non-Jew, in modern times.

Jews around the world spoke of a strange and constant tug they felt upon hearing the news of this lost girl named Suri. An Israeli man, who said he hadn't considered himself more than a Jew in name before this incident, flew to Connecticut to help in the search. He told a passenger seated beside him on the El Al Thursday evening flight from Tel Aviv, "I don't know exactly what's motivating me. Something inside me is pushing me and I'm going."

"Somehow, she awakened all these feelings," Mrs. Liba Perlow, who taught Jewish studies at the Sara Schenirer Seminary in Brooklyn at the time, said. "My fourth-grade son told me a boy in his class couldn't sleep all night, he was worried so much. My 11th grade daughter was praying like it was Yom Kippur. All the teenaged girls at school felt like it was their sister out there. Parents felt like it was their child."

In Connecticut, by nightfall Wednesday, as 90 state policemen gathered on the scene, the first group of volunteers pulled up in an ambulance and van marked Hatzoloh. Several Chassidic Jews with beards, sidelocks, and walkie-talkies climbed out and announced they were from a New York City volunteer ambulance corps and were there to help. "I told the police that they shouldn't underestimate what we can do by the way we look," Isaac Abraham, one of the volunteers, said.

In Brooklyn, an equally dramatic scene was unfolding. Shomrim, a volunteer Jewish police patrol from the Chassidic community of Williamsburg, began driving through the streets of Brooklyn with loudspeakers calling for able-bodied volunteers. By 9 p.m., 200 volunteers showed up. By 2:30 a.m., thousands of Jews of all ages, shapes and appearances clamored to board the private buses parked at 14th Avenue and 44th Street in Boro Park. The buses were equipped to carry just 250 individuals to Connecticut. The vast majority had to be turned away.

"It was such a beautiful scene," said Dovid Norman, who was a 17-year-old student at Brooklyn's Torah Temimah Yeshiva

"It was such a beautiful scene. Young students and elderly Jews with white beards waiting anxiously, hoping to get on the buses."

at the time and one of the people turned away. "Young students and elderly Jews with white beards waiting anxiously, hoping to get on the buses."

Those who didn't take part in the actual search were scrambling for other ways to help. Staff members from a Jewish school in Providence, Rhode Island drove to the site with a station wagon loaded with food – all kosher- for the volunteers, many of whom were religious Jews. Shipments of food arrived regularly.

"Two ladies from Boston brought huge bags full of fruits and nuts and explained that they weren't very religious, but they wanted to help and knew we could eat this," one of the Hatzoloh volunteers, who asked not to be named, said. Even the Hatzoloh volunteers who spend their lives dedicated to helping those in need were moved by the overwhelming response from Jewish communities spanning the Northeast as far as Canada.

The news media could not comprehend – or believe – what they were witnessing. A reporter from Rhode Island approached volunteer Leo Roth who had traveled from Brooklyn to help search for Suri. Mr. Roth, who related the story afterwards, said that the reporter asked him if he knew the Feldman family. Mr. Roth explained that he didn't; he came because the girl was a Jewish child and she was lost.

The reporter then asked Mr. Roth if he had taken off time from work to come. Mr. Roth said, yes, he and his partner had closed their electronics store so that they could help in the search. Incredulous, the reporter left to phone Mr. Roth's home in Brooklyn to verify the story with his wife. The reporter returned to Mr. Roth and told him that he had always considered himself a highly educated man; he held four degrees. The reporter said he had learned that day that "he didn't know anything," and said he felt humbled and privileged to meet Mr. Roth and those others like him.

The media were not the only ones impressed. "I have never seen a response like this," said Lt. Louis E. Lacaprucia, commanding officer of the Major Crime Squad of the Eastern District Criminal Investigation Section of the Connecticut State Police. "I have never seen such an outpouring." Lt. Lacaprucia said that before that week he had known very little about Jewish culture, but received quite an education in those agonizing three days.

Rabbi Bernard Freilich of Brooklyn's Council of Jewish Organizations said that a detective from the Connecticut State

Police told him; "I always heard of how the Jews are such a tight-knit group, but if I hadn't seen this with my own eyes, I wouldn't have believed it!"

The meeting of two cultures – the Connecticut police with hundreds of volunteers, most of them Jewish and many of them sporting full Chassidic regalia – was interesting for both parties. "We're talking about people from the northeast hills of Connecticut working side-by-side with a culture they probably only read about or maybe saw on television," Sgt. Scott R. O'Mara, public information officer of the Connecticut State Police, said. "I watched members of their (the Jewish) community coming around with sandwiches and soda, making sure that everyone was given something to eat and drink. Policemen often stand out in the field days on end and there's very few people who have that kind of concern for our well-being."

Throughout the days of searching, the Jews periodically stopped to gather together for the morning, afternoon and evening prayers. "To see people stop what they're doing and pay attention to their beliefs and immediately resume the task at hand is a lesson for all of us," Sgt. O'Mara said.

As time wore on, members of the police also began praying. "I came home on Friday and told my wife that what we need now is a miracle," Lt. Lacaprucia said. "We rely on resources such as helicopters and bloodhounds and we had simply exhausted them."

By Friday, Suri's disappearance had penetrated the public consciousness. On a New York City subway train, a woman walked over to a young Chassidic rabbi engrossed in study to tell him, "Rabbi, I don't want to disturb you, I'm not Jewish, but I want you to know that I'm also praying for that little girl." The rabbi related the story later, but asked not to be identified by name.

Classes at Tomer Devorah, the school Suri attended, could not go on as usual. All the girls could think about was Suri. Mrs. Yocheved Singer, the principal of Hebrew Studies at the school, said. In addition to praying, they offered their good deeds as a merit for her safety. "Girls who had been involved in spats decided to reconcile their differences," Mrs. Singer said. "They gave charity and prayed continually."

By Friday morning, the third day of the search, the police and volunteers had covered nearly all 25 square miles of the park and forest area and had crossed the Massachusetts border.

The police feared the worst. The volunteers, including the Orthodox Jews, were prepared to work into Shabbat to continue to search for Suri; in matters of danger to human life, if breaking the Shabbat laws became necessary, Torah law requires those laws to be broken. The police also intended to stick it out. "As long as you stay, we'll stay," Lt. Paul D. Fitzgerald of the Connecticut State Police told the volunteers.

Shortly after 10:30 a.m., John Mulcahy of Massachusetts's Southbridge Police noticed a road not marked on any of his maps. He followed it along with some of his colleagues. After a short distance, he saw a young girl beside a tree. It was Suri.

He called out to her. She remained still. Suri explained later that she was in the middle of the *Shema*, a declaration of G-d's sovereignty and unity. Throughout her 48 hours and 26 minutes alone in the woods, she had recited every prayer she remembered, she told her school principal later.

At one point in her ordeal, it had started to rain, she said. She started to panic, but remembered that a few years earlier, at that same time of year, her uncle from England had been visiting and had left her house in the rain without an umbrella. When Suri's mother ran after him to offer him one, he declined and said that the rains that fall between *Pesach* and *Shavuot* are rains of blessing. For that kind of rain, you don't need an umbrella, he said.

Suri told her family afterwards that when she remembered that, the rain became a comfort. She knew the rain would bring her blessing too, and she was sure she would be found.

If her searchers had been unified throughout her disappearance, they were even more united in their joy at her rescue. In Connecticut and Brooklyn, the volunteers could not contain their delight and san and danced rapturously. A Hatzoloh volunteer who had returned to Brooklyn watched the celebrations on a television showing a split screen of the dancing in Brooklyn and Connecticut. "I watched as a Jew hoisted the fire chief on his shoulders. They danced ecstatically together and I cried."

It is a Jewish tradition that after an individual or community survives a life-threatening crisis a special meal is prepared, in celebration and gratitude. Suri's school held this celebration in their school auditorium Thursday, May 12th, and invited Massachusetts and Connecticut's commanding policemen and others involved in the search.

Suri told her family afterwards that when she remembered that, the rain became a comfort. She knew the rain would bring her blessing too, and she was sure she would be found.

Speaker after speaker highlighted the unprecedented unity demonstrated throughout the search. It was a poignant, real-life lesson; in the school's classrooms, located just above the speakers' heads, the students learn daily about the importance of unity and the value of human life, Mrs. Singer, the principal, said. They are taught the Jewish principle that if one saves a single life, it is as if that person had saved an entire world.

Suri told Mrs. Singer that she didn't cry throughout the ordeal. The first time she cried was when she saw the video of the search and the enormity of the concern for her. She cried in gratitude, Mrs. Singer said.

Others were grateful to Suri.

"That little girl thanked the whole world for saving her life. I think we have to thank her," said Nancee France, at the time a respiratory therapy student at Rockland Community College in New York. "She brought us all together. I never saw such unity before. I never felt such unity before."

Perhaps the most dramatic demonstration of unity occurred in the closing minutes of those trying 48 hours. A vast number of Jewish schools in Brooklyn had organized a collective recitation of *Tehillim* (psalms) for Suri's safety, which began at 10:30 a.m. Friday. Suri was found 10:32 a.m.

"The Jewish people are supposed to be like one person, with one heart," said Mrs. Perlow, the teacher at the Sara Schenirer Seminary. "In Suri's rescue, we felt all our differences melt away. There were no judgments of each other, no divisiveness. One part of the Jewish people was out there, lost. We had to find her."

❧ ❧ ❧

From the Jewish Women's Journal, Summer 1994,
by Bayla S. Brenner

Ahavah — love. The root letters are הב, the Aramaic word for to give, as the more one gives the more they love the recipient.

Amalek — a descendant of Esau, who was first to wage war with the people of Israel merely because they were Jews. There is a Torah commandment to eradicate the memory of Amalek.

Avot — the fathers or Patriarchs, Abraham, Isaac and Jacob.

Avraham Avinu — Abraham, our father, one of the Partriarchs.

Beit Hamedrash — study hall, also used in conjunction with a synagogue which is used for prayer and study.

Bat Yisroel — literally, daughter of Israel. Refers to the behavior befitting a girl who embodies the positive characteristics of Judaism.

Berachot — blessings.

Bereishit, Shemot, Vayikra, Bamidbar, Devarim — the Hebrew names for the Five Books of Moses; Genesis, Exodus, Leviticus, Numbers and Deuteronomy, respectively.

Bikur Cholim — Visiting the sick. Also refers to community based groups, such as Rivkah Laufer Bikur Cholim which provide transportation to visit patients, rooms for their families, and kosher food for patients and their families.

Challah — The bread loaves eaten on Shabbat and Yom Tov. The word challah also refers to an olive-sized piece that is separated from the dough. In the time of the Holy Temple, it was given too the priest, the kohen; today it is burned.

Chassid — Adherent of a Rebbe, spiritual leader, of various groups of primarily Eastern European Orthodox Jews. Chassidism was the movement started by Rabbi Yisroel Baal Shem Tov in the 18th century.

Chinuch — the process of instructing or teaching a young child to follow a certain path in life, or to perform a certain mitzvah.

Emunah — faith, belief in G-d.

Erev Shabbat — Friday night, the eve of the Shabbat.

Gemach — an acronym for gemillat chasodim (organization), an institution that makes loans or needed items available as a community service, for little or no cost. *Gemachs* are often established in memory or in honor of an individual.

Geulah — redemption

Hashpa'ah — The influence of one person on another, either positively or negatively.

Glossary

Hashem — Literally, the Name (of G-d), a common usage of the Name of G-d which cannot be written.

Halachah — Jewish law. The immutable principles of Torah are the basis for Jewish laws as rendered by *halachic* decisors, or *poskim*. Recognized *halachic* authorities rule on every aspect of Jewish life.

Hamelech — the king, as in Dovid Hamelech, King David.

Hatzolah — A community based volunteer organization comprised of medics, paramedics and a dedicated group of trained healthcare assistants who work selflessly to save lives in an extremely expeditious fashion.

Hishtadlut — personal effort.

Imahot — The mothers, or Matriarchs, Sarah, Rebecca, Rachel and Leah.

Kavannah — concentration, particularly when relating to prayer.

Kiddush — a celebration of family and friends tendered on Shabbat in honor of the birth of a daughter or other cause for offering thanks to G-d publicly.

Kohen — a member of the priestly family, descendants of Aaron the (High) Priest.

Lashon hakodesh — the Holy Language of Hebrew, the Biblically, Divinely inspired usage as opposed to modern colloquial expression.

Maariv — the evening prayer.

Mazalot — The astrological signs of the Zodiac. Each lunar month in the Hebrew calendar has a corresponding sign.

Megillah — A scroll, usually related to a text, as in *Megillat Esther*.

Melave malkah — literally, to escort the (Shabbat) Queen, a meal held on Saturday night to bid farewell to the Shabbat.

Mesillat Yesharim — Path of the Just. Authored by Rabbi Moshe Chaim Luzzato (1707-1747), it is a classic work of ethical teachings, citing traits essential to perfecting one's character.

Midot — character traits, as in the 13 midot, or principle character traits outlined by R' Yisroel Salanter.

Midrash — The elucidation of parts of the Torah, Prophets and Writings by the Rabbis of the Mishnah. It includes allegorical interpretations, narrative commentary and statements which take the reader "between the lines" of the text.

Mincha — the afternoon prayer.

Glossary

Minchat chinuch — the inaugural offering of a *kohen* when he began his service in the Holy Temple.

Mishnah — The Oral Tradition transmitted from Moses at Mount Sinai, and redacted by Rabbi Yehudah the Prince in sapproximately 200 C.E. The Rabbis of the Mishnah were called Tannaim. The period of the Mishnah lasted approximately 400 years.

Mitzvah (pl. mitzvot) — commandment(s), either of Torah or Rabbinic origin.

Mitzvat aseh shehazman gromo — positive Torah commandments that are designated to be performed at a specific time of the day or night, or a specific time of the year.

Moshe Rabbeinu — Moses, our teacher. An exalted title given to Moses who received the Torah from G-d at Mount Sinai.

Mussar Movement — A program of study, introspection and character perfection based on Torah principles. The primary architect of this program, which became the forerunner of the style of many contemporary Yeshivot, was Reb Yisroel Salanter.

Nazir — an individual who has accepted upon himself not to cut his hair, drink wine or defile himself by being in contact with a corpse. This exalted state of sanctity lasts for as long as he specifies, or for thirty days if the vow is not specified.

Parshat hashavua — the Torah portion of the week read in the synagogue each Shabbat.

Pele Yoetz — A volume authored by Rabbi Eliezer Papo, an 18th century scholar which outlines various principles of Judaism, arranged alphabetically.

Pesikta Eicha Rabbati — A Midrashic commentary on the Book of Lamentations.

Pirkei Avot — Ethics of the Fathers. A collection of ethical teachings authored by the Sages of the Mishnah, representing Judaism's most complete compendium regarding interpersonal and intrapersonal behavior.

Rosh Chodesh — the first day (or two days) of the new Jewish(lunar) month. Before there was a fixed calendar, the new month depended on the testimony of witnesses.

Sefirah — The 49 days which are counted between Passover and Shavuot. It is also called *sefirat ha'omer* the counting from the second day of Passover when the barley *omer* offering was brought in the Temple.

Glossary

Seudat mitzvah/reshut — A festive meal held in celebration of a life cycle event. A seudat mitzvah is a Rabbinically ordained meal, while a seudat reshut is an optional celebration.

Shacharit — the morning prayer.

Shehechiyanu — A bessing recited on festivals and in celebration of mitzvot that are performed from time to time. "Blessed are You, Hashem, our G-d, King of the Universe, who has kept us alive and sustained us and enabled us to come to this season."

Shelah — Rabbi Yeshaya HaLevi Horowitz, a great 17th century Torah scholar, authored a work on the Torah, with Kabbalistic interpretations included called <u>S</u>hnay <u>L</u>uchot <u>H</u>abrit, the acronym for his name, *Shelah*.

Shema — The portion which proclaims Israel's acceptance of the sovereignty of G-d. "Hear O Israel, Hashem is our G-d, Hashem is One" (Devarim 6:4).

Shemoneh Esrei — Also called *amidah*, the eighteen blessings (later, a nineteenth was added) said as part of the daily service, three times a day. The blessings are divided into praise, requests and thanksgiving.

Siddur — Prayer book.

Targum Yonatan ben Uziel — The commentary on Torah was authored by this Tanna, from the period of the Mishnah. He was said to be the greatest of the eighty disciples of Hillel.

Tefillin — Phylacteries. Black leather boxes worn by males over thirteen years of age on the arm and on the head. They contain certain scriptural passages.

Tomchei Shabbos — A community based organization based in Boro Park, Brooklyn which delivers food parcels before Shabbat and Yom Tov in a discreet and dignified manner.

Tzaddik — A righteous, pious individual.

Tzniut — literally, modesty. This refers to the concept of looking to highlight one's inner being, and being modest in manner and dress.

Vidui — the confessional prayer recited on YomKippur.

Zohar — The mystical teachings of the Torah, compiled by the Tanna, Rabbi Shimon bar Yochai.

RABBI YONAH WEINRIB SPECIALIZES IN ELABORATE MANUSCRIPT ILLUMINATION, COMBINING RESEARCH FROM TRADITIONAL TEXTS WITH EXACTING CALLIGRAPHY AND ARTWORK. HE HAS LECTURED AND EXHIBITED INTERNATIONALLY, AND HIS WORKS ARE FOUND IN MUSEUMS, PRESTIGIOUS GALLERIES AND PRIVATE COLLECTIONS AROUND THE WORLD.

Rabbi Weinrib has illuminated and authored numerous volumes of Judaica including:

- Pirkei Avos — Collector's Edition, Deluxe leather and standard editions

- The Manuscript Shiron Series (Grace After Meals and Songs) • Bar Mitzvah Shiron • Bat Mitzvah Shiron • Wedding Shiron • The Shabbos Shiron

- Bar Mitzvah: Its Observance and Significance,

- Transitions: The Bat Mitzvah Treasury

- Hallel — Deluxe leather and standard editions

- The Haggadah in Memory of the Holocaust

- The Megillah of Redemption — Megillat Esther

- כנפי תפלה / Wings of Prayer

- Shiron Am Echad — Ashkenaz / Sepharadi Bentcher

Additionally, he has been commissioned by major Jewish organizations to create numerous presentation awards, including those for heads of state.

For more information on exhibitions, art publications or a complete catalogue of his works including framed wall hangings, contact JUDAICA ILLUMINATIONS • WWW.JUDAICAILLUMINATIONS.COM or your local Judaica bookseller.